EMPOWERING PURSUITS FOR EVERY WOMAN

UNLEASHING PASSION AND FINDING YOUR ZEN

Q.T. ARCHER

Edited, Formatted, and Cover Design by Steam Engine Publishing.

First Edition 2025

eBook ISBN 979-8-9912282-1-3
Paperback ISBN 979-8-9912282-2-0
Audiobook ISBN 979-8-9912282-3-7

For rights and permissions, please contact:

Aber Stoat Publishing, LLC
2173 Salk Ave, Ste 250
Carlsbad, CA. 92008
hello@aberstoatpublishing.com
http://aberstoatpublishing.com
@aberstoat

TABLE OF CONTENTS

INTRODUCTION

Welcome to "Empowering Pursuits for Every Woman: Unleashing Passion and Finding Your Zen." Whether you're a seasoned enthusiast of various hobbies or someone looking to rediscover the joys of personal passions, this book is your companion on a transformative journey. Life's demands can sometimes make us forget the things that truly make us feel alive, but I'm here to remind you: it's never too late to reignite that spark.

Think back to the times when you felt truly exhilarated—when you were fully immersed in an activity that made hours feel like minutes. Those moments of pure joy are not just remnants of the past. They're waiting for you right here, right now. This book is your invitation to step out of your daily routine, explore new interests, and embrace a world of possibilities that can bring fulfillment and joy.

Life is a beautiful journey, and each chapter brings new opportunities for growth and discovery. As women, we often juggle multiple roles and responsibilities, sometimes putting our own needs and passions on the back burner. But let me assure you, finding and nurturing your passions is not a luxury. It's a necessity for a balanced, fulfilling life. It's time to rediscover what sets your soul on fire and learn how to incorporate it into your daily life.

THE IMPORTANCE OF PASSION: WHY EVERY WOMAN NEEDS A HOBBY

Our passions are the compass guiding us to our true selves. Engaging in activities that excite us isn't just about passing the time. It's about enriching our lives and enhancing our overall well-being. Hobbies play a crucial role in our mental, emotional, and even physical health. They provide a sense of purpose, a break from the daily grind, and a chance to connect with others who share our interests.

Imagine this: You've always had a love for painting, but life got in the way. You prioritized career, family, and other responsibilities over your artistic inclinations. Now, you find yourself yearning for that creative outlet. Picking up a paintbrush again can be incredibly therapeutic, offering a sense of accomplishment and a way to express emotions that words often fail to capture. This is the magic of hobbies—they allow us to reconnect with parts of ourselves that might have been neglected.

But why exactly is having a hobby so important for every woman? Let's dive deeper:

MENTAL AND EMOTIONAL BENEFITS

Engaging in a hobby can significantly boost your mental health. Activities like reading, gardening, or crafting can reduce stress and anxiety, offering a peaceful escape from the hustle and bustle of everyday life. Hobbies provide a mental break, allowing your brain to shift gears and relax. They also stimulate creativity and improve cognitive functions, keeping your mind sharp and engaged.

For instance, if you've ever lost yourself in a good book, you know the feeling of being transported to another world. This not only relaxes the mind but also enhances empathy and understanding by exposing you to different perspectives. Similarly, activities like knitting or puzzle-solving require focus and concentration, which can be meditative and calming.

SOCIAL CONNECTIONS AND COMMUNITY

Pursuing a hobby often leads to new social connections. Whether you're joining a local book club, participating in a cooking class, or hiking with a group, hobbies provide opportunities to meet like-minded individuals. These social interactions are vital for our emotional well-being, offering a sense of community and belonging.

Building relationships with others who share your interests can be incredibly rewarding. It opens doors to new friendships and support networks, enriching your social life and providing a sense of camaraderie. These connections can be particularly empowering for women, offering encouragement and inspiration in a safe, supportive environment.

PHYSICAL HEALTH BENEFITS

Certain hobbies also contribute to physical health. Activities like dancing, swimming, or gardening involve physical movement, which can improve cardiovascular health, increase strength, and boost overall fitness. Even less physically demanding hobbies, such as yoga or tai chi, enhance flexibility and promote a sense of inner peace and well-being.

Physical activities also release endorphins, the body's natural mood lifters, which can help combat feelings of depression and anxiety. Engaging in regular physical activity through hobbies can lead to a healthier, more balanced lifestyle, contributing to longevity and a higher quality of life.

FINDING YOUR ZEN: THE TRANSFORMATIVE EFFECTS OF ENGAGING IN HOBBIES

While passions drive us to explore and create, finding your zen is about achieving a state of balance and tranquility in your life. Engaging in hobbies can be a powerful tool for achieving this sense of inner peace. When you immerse yourself in an activity you love, it can bring about a meditative state, reducing stress and promoting mindfulness.

MINDFULNESS AND STRESS REDUCTION

Mindfulness is the practice of being fully present in the moment, and hobbies are a natural way to cultivate this state of mind. Whether you're practicing yoga, painting, or simply taking a walk in nature, these activities encourage you to focus on the present, helping to quiet the mind and reduce the constant chatter of daily worries.

For example, gardening can be a deeply grounding activity. The act of tending to plants, feeling the soil in your hands, and observing the growth process can be incredibly calming and centering. It connects you to the rhythms of nature and provides a serene escape from the demands of modern life.

CREATIVE EXPRESSION AND EMOTIONAL RELEASE

Creative hobbies offer a unique outlet for emotional expression and release. Writing, for instance, allows you to articulate your thoughts and feelings, providing clarity and insight. Similarly, activities like painting or playing music enable you to express emotions in a non-verbal way, which can be profoundly healing.

Engaging in creative pursuits helps process emotions, release tension, and gain a deeper understanding of yourself. It's a way to communicate your inner world and find solace in the act of creation. This emotional release can lead to greater emotional resilience and a more balanced, peaceful state of mind.

PERSONAL GROWTH AND SELF-DISCOVERY

Hobbies also foster personal growth and self-discovery. Trying new activities challenges you to step out of your comfort zone, build new skills, and discover hidden talents. This journey of exploration can be incredibly empowering, boosting self-confidence and opening up new avenues for personal development.

For instance, taking up a new language or learning to cook a new cuisine can be both exciting and enriching. These pursuits not only enhance your skill set but also broaden your horizons, exposing you to new cultures and perspectives. This continuous learning and growth contribute to a more fulfilling and dynamic life.

THE ROAD AHEAD: DISCOVERING YOUR PASSION

As we embark on this journey together, the first step is to discover what truly excites and inspires you. In Part I: Discovering Your Passion, we'll explore various activities and interests that can ignite your enthusiasm and bring joy to your life. We'll delve into practical tips and exercises to help you uncover your passions and integrate them into your daily routine.

Remember, this journey is uniquely yours. There's no right or wrong way to pursue your interests. The goal is to find what resonates with you and brings you happiness. Whether it's picking up a long-forgotten hobby, trying something completely new, or diving deeper into an existing passion, this book is here to guide and support you every step of the way.

So, are you ready to unleash your passion and find your zen? Let's dive in and discover the empowering pursuits that will enrich your life and lead you to a state of balance and fulfillment. The adventure begins now, and I can't wait to see where it takes you.

PART I

DISCOVERING YOUR PASSION

Embarking on the journey to discover your passion is an exhilarating adventure that holds the promise of uncovering new dimensions of yourself. Passion is the heartbeat of a fulfilling life, the spark that brings excitement and joy to our everyday experiences. In this part of the book, we will delve into the process of finding those activities and interests that truly resonate with you, bringing a sense of purpose and enthusiasm to your life.

Discovering your passion is akin to navigating uncharted waters. It requires curiosity, exploration, and a willingness to step outside your comfort zone. Many of us have buried our passions under layers of responsibilities and routine, but it's never too late to unearth them. Whether you're reigniting a long-forgotten interest or exploring something entirely new, this journey is about reconnecting with what makes you feel alive.

Imagine your passion as a compass, guiding you toward a more vibrant and fulfilling life. This compass isn't just about finding hobbies, it's about identifying what genuinely excites you and aligns with your values and desires. It's about creating a life filled with moments that spark joy and feed your soul. This journey starts with a single step: the decision to explore and discover.

To start, we'll introduce the "Passion Compass" method, a tool designed to help you navigate the vast sea of possibilities and find the perfect hobby that aligns with your interests and values. This method will serve as your guide, helping you pinpoint activities that not only bring you joy but also enrich your life in meaningful ways.

The "Passion Compass" method is about more than just choosing a hobby. It's about understanding yourself on a deeper level. What activities make you lose track of time? What pursuits leave you feeling energized and fulfilled? By answering these questions and more, you'll begin to chart a course toward a hobby that truly resonates with your inner self.

The process involves reflecting on your interests, experimenting with different activities, and paying attention to what truly excites you. It's a journey of self-discovery that requires patience and an open mind. By the end of this section, you'll have a clearer understanding of what you're passionate about and how to incorporate those passions into your daily life.

In the subsequent subsections, we'll explore various ways to reconnect with your passions and overcome any barriers that might stand in your way. From tapping into the joys of your childhood to taking a hobby personality test, each step is designed to bring you closer to discovering what makes your heart sing.

So, are you ready to embark on this exciting journey? Let's dive into the first step and explore the "Passion Compass" method, your guide to navigating the way to the perfect hobby.

CHAPTER 1

THE "PASSION COMPASS" METHOD: NAVIGATING YOUR WAY TO THE PERFECT HOBBY

Discovering your passion can feel like an overwhelming task, but it doesn't have to be. The "Passion Compass" method is a simple yet powerful tool designed to help you navigate the myriad possibilities and pinpoint the hobbies that will bring you the most joy and fulfillment. This method combines self-reflection, exploration, and a bit of experimentation to guide you toward your ideal hobby.

STEP 1: REFLECT ON YOUR INTERESTS AND VALUES

The first step in the "Passion Compass" method is to take a moment to reflect on your interests and values. What activities have you enjoyed in the past? What topics or activities consistently capture your attention? Think about the things that make you lose track of time, the activities that leave you feeling energized and inspired.

Grab a journal and start writing down your thoughts. Consider the following questions to help guide your reflection:

- What did you love to do as a child?
- What activities make you feel happy and fulfilled?
- Are there any skills or talents that come naturally to you?

- What topics or activities do you find yourself gravitating toward in your free time?
- What causes or values are you passionate about?

By reflecting on these questions, you'll start to uncover patterns and themes that can point you toward potential hobbies. Remember, this process is about self-discovery, so there's no right or wrong answer. The goal is to get a clearer picture of what excites and motivates you.

STEP 2: EXPLORE DIFFERENT ACTIVITIES

Once you have a list of potential interests, it's time to explore different activities. This is where the fun begins! Start by picking a few activities from your list and trying them out. The key here is to keep an open mind and be willing to step out of your comfort zone. You might discover a passion for something unexpected.

Consider joining local clubs or groups that focus on your interests. Many communities offer classes or workshops on a variety of topics, from cooking and painting to hiking and photography. These opportunities not only allow you to try new activities but also connect you with like-minded individuals who share your interests.

Here are a few ideas to get you started:

- **Creative Pursuits**: Try painting, drawing, writing, or crafting. Creative hobbies allow you to express yourself and can be incredibly therapeutic.
- **Physical Activities**: Explore yoga, dance, hiking, or cycling. Physical hobbies keep you active and improve your overall well-being.
- **Intellectual Interests**: Dive into reading, puzzles, learning a new language, or studying a subject that fascinates you. Intellectual hobbies stimulate your mind and keep you curious.

- **Social Activities**: Join a book club, cooking class, or volunteer group. Social hobbies help you connect with others and build a sense of community.

STEP 3: PAY ATTENTION TO YOUR REACTIONS

As you try out different activities, pay close attention to your reactions. How do you feel during and after each activity? Do you feel energized and excited, or do you feel indifferent and bored? Your emotional response is a powerful indicator of whether an activity aligns with your passions.

Keep a journal of your experiences, noting what you enjoyed and what you didn't. This will help you narrow down your options and identify the activities that truly resonate with you. Remember, it's okay if not every activity sparks joy. The goal is to explore and find what truly excites you.

STEP 4: GIVE YOURSELF PERMISSION TO EXPERIMENT

One of the biggest barriers to discovering your passion is the fear of failure or the belief that you need to find the "perfect" hobby right away. Give yourself permission to experiment and make mistakes. The journey to finding your passion is rarely a straight path, and it's important to approach it with a sense of curiosity and playfulness.

Allow yourself to try new things without the pressure of perfection. Embrace the process of discovery and enjoy the journey. You might find that your passions evolve over time, and that's perfectly okay. The important thing is to stay open and keep exploring.

STEP 5: INTEGRATE YOUR PASSION INTO YOUR DAILY LIFE

Once you've identified a few activities that you enjoy, find ways to integrate them into your daily life. Carving out time for your hobbies can be challenging, especially with a busy schedule, but it's essential for your well-being. Make a commitment to yourself to prioritize your passions, even if it's just a few minutes each day.

Consider creating a dedicated space in your home for your hobby, whether it's a cozy reading nook, a craft corner, or a yoga mat in the living room. Having a designated space can make it easier to incorporate your hobbies into your routine.

STEP 6: SHARE YOUR PASSION WITH OTHERS

Sharing your passion with others can enhance your experience and provide a sense of community. Whether it's joining a club, attending workshops, or simply talking about your hobbies with friends and family, sharing your interests can deepen your connection to your passions.

Consider finding a hobby buddy—someone who shares your interests and can join you in your activities. Having a partner can make the experience more enjoyable and provide motivation and support.

STEP 7: REEVALUATE AND ADJUST

As you continue to explore and integrate your hobbies into your life, take time to reevaluate and adjust as needed. Your interests and passions may evolve, and that's perfectly normal. Periodically reflect on your experiences and make changes to keep your hobbies aligned with your current interests and lifestyle.

Remember, the "Passion Compass" method is a tool to guide you on your journey. It's not about finding a single, definitive passion but about discovering and nurturing activities that bring joy and fulfillment to your life. The journey itself is a rewarding experience, filled with opportunities for growth and self-discovery.

Now that we've explored the "Passion Compass" method and laid the groundwork for discovering your perfect hobby, let's delve into a delightful aspect of passion exploration—reconnecting with your inner child. Often, the activities that brought us joy in childhood hold the key to our deepest interests and desires. Let's take a nostalgic journey back to those carefree days and see how our childhood joys can illuminate the path to our adult passions in the next section, "Unleashing Your Inner Child: Reconnecting with Childhood Joys."

CHAPTER 2

UNLEASHING YOUR INNER CHILD: RECONNECTING WITH CHILDHOOD JOYS

Remember the days when every backyard was a kingdom waiting to be explored, every cardboard box a spaceship bound for distant galaxies? Childhood is a time of unbridled imagination and boundless curiosity—a time when play was serious business and joy was found in the simplest of moments. As adults, we often lose touch with the magic of those early years, consumed instead by responsibilities and routines.

But what if we could tap into that reservoir of childhood wonder once more? What if we could rediscover the activities that made our hearts sing and our spirits soar? Reconnecting with your inner child isn't just about nostalgia—it's about reclaiming a sense of playfulness, curiosity, and creativity that can enrich every aspect of your life.

EMBRACING PLAYFULNESS AND CURIOSITY

Think back to the activities that brought you joy as a child. Whether it was building sandcastles at the beach, climbing trees in the backyard, or staging epic adventures with your favorite toys, these experiences hold clues to your deepest passions. Embracing your inner child means giving yourself permission to explore without boundaries, to embrace the joy of discovery in everyday moments.

REDISCOVERING FORGOTTEN PASSIONS

Life has a way of steering us away from the activities that once brought us joy. Maybe you loved to draw, sing, or play a musical instrument. Perhaps you spent hours lost in books or exploring nature. Reconnecting with your inner child involves revisiting these forgotten passions, allowing yourself to indulge in activities that ignite your imagination and fill your heart with happiness.

CULTIVATING CREATIVITY AND IMAGINATION

Creativity is the lifeblood of childhood—a world where anything is possible and the ordinary becomes extraordinary. Engaging in creative pursuits as an adult not only sparks inspiration but also nurtures a sense of self-expression and emotional well-being. Whether you're painting, writing, gardening, or crafting, creative hobbies allow you to tap into your innermost thoughts and feelings, fostering a deeper connection to yourself and the world around you.

FINDING JOY IN SIMPLE PLEASURES

Children find joy in the simplest of pleasures—a butterfly fluttering by, a puddle to jump in, a kite dancing in the sky. Reconnecting with your inner child means slowing down and appreciating the beauty and wonder that surround you every day. It's about rediscovering the magic in small moments and cultivating a sense of gratitude for the present.

EMBRACING A SENSE OF WONDER AND ADVENTURE

Childhood is synonymous with adventure—exploring new places, trying new things, and embracing the unknown with fearless curiosity. Reconnecting with your inner child means reclaiming that sense of wonder and excitement in your adult life. Whether it's traveling to new destinations, learning a new skill, or embarking on a spontaneous adventure, allow yourself to step outside your comfort zone and embrace the thrill of exploration.

As we've explored the joys of reconnecting with our inner child and rediscovering the activities that once brought us boundless happiness, it's clear that our childhood passions hold valuable insights into our true selves. Just as our childhood experiences shape who we are today, our unique traits and personalities play a crucial role in determining the hobbies that bring us the most joy and fulfillment. In the next section, "The Hobby Personality Test: Identifying Hobbies That Suit Your Unique Traits," we'll delve into a fascinating exploration of how understanding your personality can guide you to hobbies that align perfectly with your interests and preferences. Let's embark on this journey of self-discovery and uncover the hobbies that will ignite your passion and bring you closer to living your best life.

CHAPTER 3

THE HOBBY PERSONALITY TEST: IDENTIFYING HOBBIES THAT SUIT YOUR UNIQUE TRAITS

Discovering the perfect hobby is like finding a key to unlock a world of joy and fulfillment tailored just for you. In this section, we embark on a journey of self-discovery through the Hobby Personality Test—a comprehensive tool designed to illuminate the hobbies that resonate deeply with your personality, interests, and lifestyle preferences.

UNDERSTANDING YOUR PERSONALITY LANDSCAPE

Our personalities are intricate landscapes, shaped by traits that influence how we engage with the world around us. The Hobby Personality Test begins by exploring these traits, highlighting key dimensions such as extraversion, openness to experience, conscientiousness, agreeableness, and emotional stability. Each trait offers valuable insights into the types of activities that align with our intrinsic motivations and bring us a sense of fulfillment.

For example, individuals high in extraversion may thrive in social hobbies like team sports, group fitness classes, or community volunteering. These activities provide opportunities for social interaction, collaboration, and shared achievement—qualities that resonate deeply with extraverted personalities seeking connection and camaraderie.

On the other hand, those with a high openness to experience may find fulfillment in creative pursuits such as painting, writing, playing a musical instrument, or exploring new cultures through travel. These hobbies stimulate imagination, foster innovation, and satisfy the intellectual curiosity inherent in individuals who embrace novelty and diversity.

THE HOBBY PERSONALITY TEST

Take a moment to answer the following questions honestly. Your responses will help identify hobbies that align best with your unique traits and preferences.

Social Preferences: How much do you enjoy socializing and being around others?

    A. Love it! I thrive in social settings.
    B. It's enjoyable, but I also value alone time.
    C. I prefer solitary activities.

Adventure and Novelty: How open are you to trying new things and exploring unfamiliar territories?

    A. Very open! I love seeking out new experiences.
    B. Somewhat open. I enjoy a balance of familiar and new.
    C. I prefer sticking to what I know.

Creativity and Expression: Do you find joy in creative pursuits or expressing yourself artistically?

    A. Absolutely! Creativity fuels me.
    B. Sometimes, when the mood strikes.
    C. Not particularly. I prefer practical activities.

Physical Engagement: How important is physical activity and movement to you?

    A. Vital! I need to move and stay active.
    B. Moderately important. I enjoy staying fit.
    C. Not a priority for me.

Intellectual Stimulation: Are you drawn to activities that challenge your mind and expand your knowledge?

    A. Yes, I thrive on intellectual challenges.
    B. Occasionally, if it's something I find interesting.
    C. Not particularly. I prefer straightforward tasks.

Relaxation and Stress Relief: How do you typically unwind and relax?

    A. Engaging in calming activities like meditation or yoga.
    B. Pursuing hobbies that distract and entertain me.
    C. I find relaxation in routine and familiar activities.

Practical Considerations: What practical factors influence your choice of hobbies?

    A. Time availability and flexibility are key factors.
    B. Cost and accessibility are important considerations.
    C. I prioritize hobbies that align with my lifestyle and responsibilities.

Emotional Connection: Do you seek hobbies that foster emotional connection and fulfillment?

    A. Yes, connecting with others through shared interests is important.
    B. It's nice to have, but not essential.

C. I prefer hobbies that are more personal and introspective.

Scoring:
Count the number of A's, B's, and C's you selected for each question.

Results:
- **A's:** You thrive on adventure and variety. Consider hobbies like hiking, photography, group fitness classes, or volunteering.
- **B's:** You enjoy a balanced approach. Explore hobbies such as gardening, cooking, painting, or book clubs.
- **C's:** You prefer stability and routine. Opt for hobbies like knitting, journaling, walking, or solo reading.

ALIGNING INTERESTS AND PASSIONS

Interests and passions serve as guiding stars, illuminating the path to hobbies that bring us joy and satisfaction. By identifying activities that align with your passions, you can cultivate hobbies that not only entertain but also enrich your life on a deeper level.

Consider someone with a deep passion for nature and the outdoors. Hobbies such as hiking, gardening, birdwatching, or landscape photography may hold particular appeal, providing opportunities to connect with the natural world, explore new environments, and appreciate the beauty of our planet.

LEVERAGING STRENGTHS AND SKILLS

Each of us possesses unique strengths and skills waiting to be nurtured through hobbies. Whether you excel in problem-solving, creativity, physical agility, or emotional intelligence, your hobbies can serve as a platform for personal growth and self-expression. The Hobby Personality Test helps you identify areas where you excel and suggests hobbies that allow you to leverage your strengths, build competence, and achieve personal milestones.

For example, individuals with strong analytical skills may find fulfillment in hobbies that require strategic thinking, such as chess, puzzle-solving, or coding. Engaging in these activities provides mental stimulation, challenges cognitive abilities, and fosters a sense of accomplishment through mastering complex tasks.

EMBRACING LIFESTYLE AND PRACTICALITY

While passion fuels our hobbies, practical considerations such as time availability, financial resources, physical abilities, and geographical location also play crucial roles in our choices. The Hobby Personality Test takes these factors into account, guiding you toward hobbies that fit seamlessly into your lifestyle and are sustainable in the long term. Whether you're balancing work, family, and social commitments or navigating personal challenges, finding hobbies that complement your lifestyle ensures continued engagement and enjoyment.

PERSONALIZING YOUR HOBBY JOURNEY

Personalization is key to maintaining enthusiasm and commitment to hobbies over time. As our interests evolve and life circumstances change, our hobbies can adapt to reflect these shifts. The Hobby Personality Test encourages ongoing exploration and adaptation, allowing you to tailor your hobby experiences to align with new goals, interests, and aspirations. Whether you're deepening your expertise in a familiar hobby or exploring new avenues of interest, personalizing your hobby journey ensures continued growth, fulfillment, and joy.

CONNECTING PASSION TO PURPOSE

Ultimately, our hobbies have the power to enrich our lives in profound ways—fostering personal growth, well-being, and meaningful connections with communities and causes we care about. The Hobby Personality Test illuminates the intersection of passion and purpose, guiding you toward hobbies that not only bring you joy but also align with your values and aspirations. By exploring hobbies that resonate with your personality, interests, and strengths, you can cultivate a life filled with meaning, fulfillment, and authentic self-expression.

As we've explored the intricate landscape of personality and its influence on hobby selection, it's clear that self-discovery is a catalyst for personal growth and enrichment. However, embarking on new pursuits can often be accompanied by challenges and self-doubt. In the next section, we'll delve into practical strategies for overcoming barriers and empowering yourself to embrace hobbies that bring joy and fulfillment. Let's harness the insights gained from our Hobby Personality Test and continue our journey of exploration and discovery.

CHAPTER 4

OVERCOMING BARRIERS: CONQUERING SELF-DOUBT AND EMBRACING NEW PURSUITS

Embarking on a journey to discover new passions and hobbies can be exhilarating, but it's not without its challenges. Self-doubt, fear of failure, and practical obstacles often stand in the way of pursuing activities that ignite our souls. In this section, we'll explore practical strategies to overcome these barriers and empower yourself to embrace new pursuits wholeheartedly.

EMBRACING SELF-COMPASSION

Before diving into strategies for overcoming external challenges, it's essential to address the internal barriers that may hinder our progress. Self-doubt and perfectionism are common stumbling blocks that can sap our motivation and prevent us from exploring new hobbies. Embracing self-compassion is the first step toward dismantling these barriers.

Self-compassion involves treating yourself with kindness and understanding, especially when faced with setbacks or challenges. Instead of harsh self-criticism, acknowledge that learning new skills and exploring unfamiliar territory naturally involves ups and downs. Celebrate your courage to try something new, regardless of initial outcomes.

SETTING REALISTIC EXPECTATIONS

One of the primary sources of self-doubt stems from setting unrealistic expectations for ourselves. It's crucial to recognize that mastery in any hobby takes time, patience, and persistence. Begin with realistic goals that allow for gradual progress and learning. Break down larger objectives into smaller, manageable steps to build confidence and momentum.

For instance, if you're learning a musical instrument, start with basic chords or scales before attempting more complex pieces. By celebrating each small achievement along the way, you reinforce your commitment and capability to excel in your chosen pursuit.

CULTIVATING A GROWTH MINDSET

Adopting a growth mindset is instrumental in overcoming self-doubt and embracing new challenges. Unlike a fixed mindset that believes abilities are innate and unchangeable, a growth mindset thrives on the belief that skills and talents can be developed through dedication and effort. This shift in perspective empowers you to view setbacks as opportunities for growth and learning.

When faced with challenges in your hobbies, remind yourself that every obstacle is a chance to improve and refine your skills. Seek out feedback from mentors or peers to gain valuable insights and perspectives. Embrace the process of learning and view mistakes as valuable lessons that contribute to your overall development.

MANAGING TIME AND PRIORITIES

Balancing new hobbies with existing responsibilities can be daunting, leading to feelings of overwhelm and hesitation. Effectively managing your time and priorities is essential to maintain consistency and enjoyment in your pursuits. Start by assessing your current commitments and identifying pockets of time that can be dedicated to your hobbies.

Consider incorporating your hobby into your daily or weekly routine to establish a sense of continuity and progress. Break down your schedule into manageable blocks of time dedicated solely to pursuing your passion. By prioritizing self-care and personal growth through hobbies, you enhance your overall well-being and resilience in managing life's demands.

BUILDING A SUPPORTIVE NETWORK

Surrounding yourself with a supportive network of like-minded individuals can significantly boost your confidence and motivation in pursuing new hobbies. Seek out communities, clubs, or online forums where you can connect with others who share your interests and goals. Engaging in discussions, sharing experiences, and seeking advice from peers create a sense of camaraderie and encouragement.

Having a support system provides valuable emotional and practical support during challenging times. Celebrate your successes together, exchange ideas, and learn from each other's experiences. Building connections within your hobby community fosters a sense of belonging and reinforces your commitment to personal growth and fulfillment.

NAVIGATING PRACTICAL CHALLENGES

Practical considerations such as financial constraints, access to resources, or physical limitations can pose significant challenges in pursuing hobbies. However, creativity and resourcefulness can help overcome these obstacles. Explore affordable or free alternatives to costly equipment or materials. Look for local community centers, libraries, or online tutorials that offer resources and support for beginners.

Adaptability is key to navigating practical challenges effectively. Consider exploring hobbies that require minimal resources or can be practiced in various environments. Embrace the opportunity to innovate and find creative solutions that align with your goals and circumstances. By focusing on the essence of your hobby and adapting to changing conditions, you maintain enthusiasm and commitment over time.

EMBRACING RESILIENCE AND PERSISTENCE

Above all, cultivating resilience and persistence is essential on your journey to discovering and nurturing your passions. Recognize that setbacks and obstacles are inevitable in any pursuit, but they do not define your ability to succeed. Embrace challenges as opportunities to build resilience and deepen your commitment to personal growth.

Practice self-reflection and celebrate your progress, no matter how small. Cultivate a sense of optimism and resilience in the face of adversity. Remember that every step forward, no matter how incremental, contributes to your overall development and fulfillment. By embracing resilience and persistence, you embody the courage and determination needed to overcome barriers and thrive in your hobby pursuits.

As we conclude our exploration of overcoming barriers and embracing new pursuits, remember that the journey to discovering your passions is as enriching as the destination itself. Each challenge you overcome, each skill you develop, and each moment of self-discovery contributes to your personal growth and fulfillment.

In the next part of our journey, Part II: Creative Pursuits for the Soul, we will delve into a diverse array of creative hobbies that inspire and nourish the spirit. From artistic endeavors to innovative projects, we will explore how these pursuits foster creativity, self-expression, and a deeper connection to our inner selves. Let's continue our exploration of passions and embrace the transformative power of creativity in our lives.

PART II

CREATIVE PURSUITS
FOR THE SOUL

Welcome to Part II of our journey together, where we'll dive into the vibrant world of creative pursuits that nourish the soul. If you've ever felt a spark of curiosity about expressing yourself through art, writing, or crafting, you're in for a treat. This section is all about unleashing your inner artist and finding joy in the process of creation.

Let's face it—we all have a creative side, even if we don't always recognize it. Maybe you doodle during phone calls, hum tunes in the shower, or come up with clever solutions to everyday problems. That's creativity in action! The chapters ahead will help you tap into that natural wellspring of imagination and use it to enrich your life in ways you might never have expected.

Think of creativity as a muscle. The more you use it, the stronger it gets. And just like exercise, creative pursuits can be a fantastic way to de-stress, boost your mood, and gain a sense of accomplishment. Whether you're painting a masterpiece or simply arranging flowers in a vase, the act of creating something beautiful or meaningful can be incredibly fulfilling.

But here's the best part—you don't need to be a pro to reap the benefits of creative hobbies. This section is all about the joy of the process, not perfection. We'll explore activities that are accessible to everyone, regardless of experience or natural talent. From the meditative practice of adult coloring books to the tactile pleasure of molding clay, there's something here for every taste and skill level.

As we journey through these chapters, you'll discover how creative pursuits can become powerful tools for self-expression, emotional release, and personal growth. We'll look at how writing can help you process your thoughts and feelings, how cooking can be a form of edible art, and how crafts like knitting can create a sense of calm and focus.

You might be surprised to find that many of these activities have roots in ancient practices or modern therapy techniques. For example, art therapy has been used to help people work through trauma, while mindfulness-based practices like Zen gardens have been promoting inner peace for centuries. By engaging in these pursuits, you're not just having fun—you're tapping into time-honored methods of nurturing your mental and emotional well-being.

So, are you ready to embark on this colorful adventure? Great! Let's kick things off by exploring the "Artist Within" technique. This powerful approach will help you unlock the creative potential that's been hiding inside you all along. Whether you consider yourself "artistic" or not, you're about to discover talents and passions you never knew you had. Turn the page, and let's begin the exciting process of unleashing your inner artist!

CHAPTER 5

THE "ARTIST WITHIN" TECHNIQUE: UNLOCKING YOUR HIDDEN CREATIVE TALENTS

Ever heard someone say, "I'm just not the creative type"? Well, I'm here to let you in on a little secret: that's a myth! Creativity isn't some magical gift bestowed upon a chosen few. It's a skill that lives inside all of us, waiting to be awakened and nurtured. The "Artist Within" technique is all about coaxing out that inner creativity, no matter how deeply it might be buried.

EMBRACING YOUR CREATIVE SPIRIT

So, what exactly is this technique? At its core, it's a set of mindsets and practices designed to help you tap into your natural creative abilities. It's about silencing your inner critic, embracing experimentation, and finding joy in the process of creation.

Remember when you were a kid, fearlessly scribbling with crayons or building fantastical worlds with blocks? That's the spirit we're aiming to recapture. The beginner's mind is all about approaching creative activities with curiosity and openness, free from the pressure of expectations.

Try this: Pick up a pen and doodle for five minutes without judging what comes out. Let your hand wander freely across the paper. It doesn't matter if you draw stick figures or abstract squiggles—the point is to enjoy the act of creating without worrying about the result.

As adults, we often get caught up in being "productive" all the time. But play is essential for creativity! It allows us to explore, take risks, and stumble upon new ideas. Set aside 15 minutes for a creative "play date" with yourself. Choose any medium—paint, clay, even digital art apps—and just have fun with it. The only rule is there are no rules!

OVERCOMING CREATIVE BLOCKS

Perfectionism is creativity's worst enemy. It keeps us from starting projects or finishing them because we're afraid they won't be "good enough." The Artist Within technique encourages you to celebrate imperfections as part of the creative process. Remember this mantra: "Done is better than perfect."

Creativity often springs from really seeing the world around us. Take time each day to notice details you might normally overlook— the play of light and shadow, the texture of tree bark, the way people move and interact. Spend five minutes describing an everyday object in as much detail as possible. You'll be amazed at how this simple exercise can sharpen your powers of observation and fuel your creativity.

Pay attention to what sparks your interest, even if it seems silly or impractical. That random fascination with cloud shapes or vintage postcards might lead to your next creative breakthrough! Make a list of five things you're curious about but have never explored. Pick one and spend some time researching or experimenting with it this week.

Sometimes, the hardest part is just getting started. If you're feeling stuck, try setting a timer for just five minutes and commit to working on your creative project for that short time. Often, you'll find that once you begin, the ideas start flowing and you'll want to continue beyond those initial five minutes.

NURTURING YOUR CREATIVE PRACTICE

Some of the most innovative ideas come from combining different fields or concepts. Don't be afraid to mix things up! Take two unrelated hobbies or interests and brainstorm ways to combine them. Love gardening and mystery novels? Maybe you could write a story about a detective who solves crimes using plant knowledge!

Surround yourself with things that ignite your imagination. This could be a physical mood board, a digital Pinterest board, or even a box of interesting objects. Start your own inspiration collection this week. Include images, quotes, textures—anything that speaks to you creatively.

Schedule time for creativity like you would any other important appointment. These regular sessions help build your creative muscles and make creativity a habit. Block out at least 30 minutes twice a week for your "creative dates." Use this time to explore any artistic pursuit that calls to you.

Sometimes, having unlimited options can be paralyzing. Giving yourself some constraints can actually boost creativity by forcing you to think outside the box. Try this challenge: Pick a color and create something using only shades of that color. Or write a story using only 50 words.

Sharing your creations can be scary, but it's also incredibly rewarding. It connects you with like-minded people and can provide motivation to keep creating. Start small by sharing one piece of your work with a trusted friend or family member this month.

Remember, creativity isn't just about making art. It's a way of thinking that can enhance every aspect of your life. Here are some ways to infuse creativity into your daily routine:

- Cook a meal without a recipe, using whatever ingredients you have on hand
- Rearrange the furniture in a room to give it a fresh feel
- Take a different route to work and notice new details about your surroundings
- Brainstorm unconventional solutions to a problem at work or home
- Write a short story inspired by an overheard conversation

The goal of the Artist Within technique isn't to make you a professional artist overnight. It's about rediscovering the joy of creation and allowing yourself to express your unique voice through various creative outlets. As you practice these techniques, you'll likely find that creativity starts spilling over into other areas of your life—problem-solving at work, coming up with fun family activities, or even how you dress and decorate your home.

The most important thing is to be patient and kind to yourself as you embark on this creative journey. Some days, ideas will flow easily. Other days, you might feel stuck. That's all part of the process! The key is to keep showing up and giving yourself the chance to create.

Remember, your creativity is like a muscle—the more you use it, the stronger it becomes. Don't be discouraged if your early attempts don't meet your expectations. Every creative master started as a beginner. What matters is that you're exploring, experimenting, and expressing yourself.

As you continue to nurture your inner artist, you might find yourself drawn to specific forms of creative expression. In our next chapter, we'll dive into the wonderful world of painting and drawing. These versatile mediums offer endless possibilities for self-expression, whether you prefer bold, abstract strokes or detailed, realistic renderings. So grab your pencils and brushes—it's time to explore the power of visual art!

CHAPTER 6

PAINTING AND DRAWING: EXPRESSING YOURSELF THROUGH COLOR AND FORM

Welcome to the vibrant world of painting and drawing! These timeless art forms offer a wonderful way to express your inner world, capture the beauty around you, and simply have fun with color and shape. Don't worry if you've never considered yourself "artistic"—this chapter is all about discovering the joy of creating visual art, regardless of your skill level.

GETTING STARTED: CHOOSING YOUR MEDIUM

Let's start with the basics. Painting and drawing are incredibly versatile mediums. You can use them to create anything from quick sketches to elaborate masterpieces. The best part? You don't need fancy equipment to get started. A simple set of pencils or watercolors can open up a whole new world of creative possibilities.

When it comes to choosing your medium, you've got plenty of options. Pencil drawing is great for beginners—all you need is a pencil and paper to start sketching. If you're looking for rich, dramatic tones, charcoal might be your thing. Watercolor offers dreamy, translucent qualities perfect for landscapes. Acrylic paint is versatile and fast-drying, good for both beginners and experienced artists. And if you're after rich colors and blending abilities, oil paint might be your go-to, though it takes longer to dry.

Don't feel like you have to commit to just one! Part of the fun is experimenting with different mediums to see what resonates with you. Try them all if you like—you might be surprised by which one speaks to you.

FINDING INSPIRATION AND OVERCOMING CHALLENGES

Now, you might be wondering, "What should I draw or paint?" The answer is simple: anything that interests you! Nature is always a great source of inspiration. Why not try capturing the flowers in your garden or the view from your window? Or arrange some everyday objects for a still life painting. People make fascinating subjects too—give portraiture a go, even if you start with stick figures. And don't forget the power of your imagination! Abstract art lets you express emotions through color and form, while painting scenes from your dreams can lead to some truly unique creations.

Remember, there are no rules about what makes a "good" subject. If it catches your eye or sparks your curiosity, it's worth exploring on paper or canvas.

As you dive into painting and drawing, you'll discover all sorts of fun techniques to try. Contour drawing, where you draw an object without looking at your paper, is a great way to train your eye and hand coordination. Playing with color mixing is like cooking, but with paint—you get to create your own unique palette. Shading helps bring depth and dimension to your work, while perspective drawing creates the illusion of 3D space on a 2D surface.

Now, let's talk about some common challenges you might face. Maybe you're frustrated because your art doesn't look "realistic" enough. Here's a secret: perfect realism isn't the goal (unless you want it to be). Many beloved artists, from Picasso to Monet, became famous for their unique interpretations of reality. Focus on developing your own style rather than achieving photographic perfection.

Feeling stumped about how to start? Sometimes a blank canvas can be intimidating. Try starting with a light sketch to map out your composition. Or simply make a mark—any mark—to break the "spell" of the white page. And don't worry about making "mistakes." In art, there are no mistakes, only opportunities. That unexpected line or color splotch might lead you in an exciting new direction. Embrace the unpredictable nature of creating!

MAKING TIME FOR ART AND EXPLORING ITS BENEFITS

Finding time for painting and drawing can be challenging in our busy lives. Here are some tips to help you carve out creative time:

- Keep a small sketchbook with you for quick doodles during downtime.
- Set up a dedicated art space, even if it's just a corner of a room.
- Schedule "art dates" with yourself or friends.
- Try the "15-minute rule"—commit to creating for just 15 minutes a day.

You'd be surprised how much you can accomplish in short, consistent bursts.

As you explore painting and drawing, you might find inspiration in different art movements. Take some time to learn about styles like Impressionism, Cubism, Pop Art, and Surrealism. You might discover a style that resonates with you or inspires you to create something entirely new!

Beyond being a fun hobby, painting and drawing can have real benefits for your mental and emotional well-being. Creating art can reduce stress and anxiety, improve focus and concentration, boost self-esteem, provide a healthy outlet for emotions, and encourage mindfulness. So the next time you're feeling overwhelmed or stuck, try picking up a pencil or brush. You might be surprised at how calming and centering it can be.

As you become more comfortable with your artistic practice, you might want to share your creations with others. This can be both exciting and nerve-wracking! Remember, art is subjective, and what matters most is how the process makes you feel. If you do decide to share, start small, perhaps with close friends or family. Consider joining a local art group or online community for support and feedback. Be open to constructive criticism, but don't let it dampen your enthusiasm. And most importantly, celebrate your progress! Compare your current work to where you started, not to professional artists.

Remember, the joy of painting and drawing lies in the process, not just the final product. Every stroke of the pencil or brush is an opportunity to express yourself, learn something new, and connect with your inner creativity. So go ahead—pick up that paintbrush or pencil and see where it takes you!

As you continue to explore the world of visual art, you might find that you're eager to express yourself in other ways too. In our next chapter, we'll dive into the powerful realm of writing as a form of creative expression and emotional release. Whether you're drawn to journaling, poetry, or storytelling, the written word offers yet another beautiful avenue for unleashing your creativity and nurturing your soul. So keep those creative juices flowing, and let's turn the page to discover the transformative power of words!

CHAPTER 7

WRITING AS THERAPY: JOURNALING, POETRY, AND STORYTELLING FOR EMOTIONAL RELEASE

Have you ever felt a jumble of emotions swirling inside you, unsure how to make sense of them? Or maybe you've experienced something profound but struggled to put it into words? Welcome to the transformative world of writing as therapy. This chapter is all about harnessing the power of the written word to explore your inner landscape, process your experiences, and find emotional release.

THE HEALING POWER OF WORDS

Writing isn't just about creating beautiful prose or crafting bestselling novels. It's a powerful tool for self-discovery, emotional processing, and personal growth. When we put pen to paper (or fingers to keyboard), we're engaging in a dialogue with ourselves. This act of self-expression can help us make sense of our thoughts, work through challenging emotions, and gain new perspectives on our lives.

One of the best things about writing as therapy is that it's accessible to everyone. You don't need to be a "good" writer or have any special skills. All you need is a willingness to be honest with yourself and the courage to explore your inner world.

JOURNALING: YOUR PERSONAL TIME MACHINE

Let's start with journaling, perhaps the most common form of therapeutic writing. Think of your journal as a judgment-free zone where you can pour out your thoughts, feelings, and experiences without fear of criticism or consequences.

Here are a few journaling techniques to try:

- Stream of consciousness: Set a timer for 10 minutes and write whatever comes to mind, without stopping or editing.
- Gratitude journaling: Each day, write down three things you're grateful for.
- Dialogue journaling: Have a written conversation with a part of yourself, a person in your life, or even an emotion.
- Future self journaling: Write a letter to your future self, or imagine your ideal life five years from now.

Remember, there's no "right" way to journal. The key is consistency. Try to write a little bit each day, even if it's just for a few minutes. Over time, you might be surprised at the insights and patterns that emerge.

POETRY: DISTILLING EMOTIONS INTO VERSE

Poetry offers a unique way to express complex emotions and experiences. Don't worry if you've never written a poem before—this isn't about crafting perfect sonnets or haikus. It's about using the concentrated nature of poetry to tap into your feelings and experiences.

Try this exercise: Choose an emotion you're currently feeling. Now, write down five sensory details that represent that emotion (sights, sounds, smells, tastes, or textures). Use these details as the building blocks for a short poem. Don't worry about rhyme or structure—just let the words flow.

Poetry can be especially helpful for processing intense emotions or experiences that feel too overwhelming to approach head-on. By distilling your feelings into imagery and metaphor, you can explore them from a slightly removed perspective.

STORYTELLING: REWRITING YOUR NARRATIVE

We all have stories we tell ourselves about who we are and what we're capable of. Sometimes, these stories can hold us back. Therapeutic storytelling allows us to examine these narratives and potentially rewrite them in empowering ways.

Try writing a short story about a challenging experience you've had, but change the ending. How would you have liked things to turn out? What would your character (you) have needed to do differently to achieve that outcome? This exercise isn't about denying reality, but about exploring possibilities and potentially shifting your perspective on past events.

Another powerful storytelling technique is to write from different perspectives. If you're struggling with a conflict, try writing the story from the other person's point of view. This can help develop empathy and potentially provide new insights into the situation.

MAKING WRITING A REGULAR PRACTICE

Like any therapeutic tool, writing is most effective when it becomes a regular part of your routine. Here are some tips to help you establish a consistent writing practice:

- Set aside a specific time each day for writing, even if it's just for 10 minutes.
- Create a comfortable, inviting writing space.
- Experiment with different times of day to find when you're most creative or reflective.

- Try different writing tools—maybe you prefer a fancy journal and pen, or perhaps you like typing on your computer.
- Join a writing group or find an accountability partner to help you stay motivated.

Remember, the goal isn't to create polished, publishable work (unless you want to!). The power of therapeutic writing lies in the process, not the product. Be kind to yourself and resist the urge to judge or edit your writing. Let it be a space for raw, honest self-expression.

As you delve into the world of therapeutic writing, you might find that certain forms resonate more with you than others. That's perfectly okay! The beauty of this practice is that it's highly personal and adaptable to your needs and preferences.

Writing can be a powerful complement to other forms of self-care and therapy. It provides a private space for reflection and emotional release, helping you process your experiences and gain new insights into yourself and your life.

As we wrap up this chapter on the healing power of words, let's look ahead to another form of creative expression that can bring joy and relaxation into your life. In the next chapter, we'll explore the world of fiber arts, diving into the soothing rhythms of knitting, crocheting, and needlework. Get ready to discover how these timeless crafts can become a source of both creativity and calm in your busy life!

CHAPTER 8

CRAFTING BLISS: FINDING JOY IN KNITTING, CROCHETING, AND NEEDLEWORK

Welcome to the cozy, comforting world of fiber arts! In this chapter, we're going to explore how the simple act of working with yarn and thread can become a source of joy, relaxation, and creative expression. Whether you're a complete beginner or you've been crafting for years, there's always something new to discover in the realm of knitting, crocheting, and needlework.

THE MEDITATIVE MAGIC OF FIBER ARTS

Have you ever watched someone knitting and wondered how they can sit so peacefully for hours, their hands moving in a rhythmic dance? There's a reason why fiber arts have been popular for centuries - they offer a unique combination of creativity, productivity, and meditation.

When you're focused on the repetitive motions of knitting or crocheting, your mind enters a state similar to meditation. This "flow state" can reduce stress, lower blood pressure, and even help manage chronic pain. It's like a moving meditation, with the added bonus of creating something beautiful in the process!

GETTING STARTED: CHOOSING YOUR CRAFT

Let's break down the main types of fiber arts you might want to try:

- Knitting: Uses two needles to create interlocking loops of yarn. Great for making sweaters, scarves, and blankets.
- Crocheting: Uses a single hook to create loops and knots. Ideal for making lace, doilies, and three-dimensional objects like stuffed animals.
- Embroidery: Decorating fabric with needle and thread. Perfect for adding personalized touches to clothing or creating wall art.
- Cross-stitch: A type of embroidery where X-shaped stitches form a picture. Excellent for creating detailed images and text.

Don't feel pressured to choose just one! Many crafters enjoy multiple fiber arts. Start with whichever appeals to you most, and remember - it's okay to be a beginner. Everyone starts somewhere!

THE JOY OF CREATING SOMETHING TANGIBLE

In our increasingly digital world, there's something deeply satisfying about creating something you can hold in your hands. Whether it's a cozy scarf, a decorative pillow, or a piece of embroidered art, fiber arts allow you to transform simple materials into objects of beauty and usefulness.

This tangible creativity can be especially rewarding when you're making gifts for others. Imagine the joy of wrapping a loved one in a blanket you knitted yourself, or seeing your embroidered art hanging on a friend's wall. These handmade items carry a piece of your time, effort, and love - making them truly special.

One of the best things about fiber arts is the supportive community that surrounds them. Local yarn shops often offer classes and knitting circles. Online tutorials and video courses can teach you new techniques from the comfort of your home. Crafting websites like

Ravelry.com offer patterns, forums, and ways to connect with other crafters. Libraries often have books on various fiber arts techniques and patterns.

Remember, everyone was a beginner once. Don't be afraid to ask for help or advice - most crafters are delighted to share their knowledge and passion!

Fiber arts offer a unique opportunity to practice mindfulness. As you work, try to focus on the sensations: the feel of the yarn or fabric, the sound of the needles clicking, the sight of the pattern emerging. This focus on the present moment can be incredibly calming and grounding.

You can even incorporate intentional mindfulness into your crafting. Some people like to say a mantra or set an intention with each stitch. Others use their crafting time for reflection or problem-solving. The repetitive nature of these crafts provides a perfect backdrop for this kind of mental work.

Like any skill, fiber arts can sometimes be frustrating. You might tangle your yarn, lose count of your stitches, or find that your finished product doesn't look quite like you imagined. These moments are all part of the learning process!

Remember, perfection isn't the goal. Each "mistake" is an opportunity to learn and improve. Many experienced crafters will tell you that it's the little imperfections that make handmade items special. They're a reminder that a real person, not a machine, created this item with love and care.

Many crafters find additional joy in using their skills to help others. There are numerous charities that accept handmade items like blankets for hospitals, hats for cancer patients, or warm clothing for homeless shelters. This can add an extra layer of meaning to your crafting, knowing that your creations will bring comfort to someone in need.

As you explore the world of fiber arts, you'll likely discover that it's about much more than just creating objects. It's about patience, perseverance, and the joy of learning. It's about connecting with a rich history of craft and with a community of fellow makers. Most of all, it's about carving out a space in your life for creativity, mindfulness, and joy.

So pick up those needles, thread that yarn, and see where your creativity takes you. You might just find that the simple act of looping yarn can lead to a whole new world of relaxation and self-expression.

Speaking of relaxation, in our next chapter, we'll explore another calming creative pursuit that's gained popularity in recent years. Get ready to dive into the world of adult coloring books, where the simple act of filling in shapes with color becomes a powerful tool for stress relief and mindfulness. It's time to rediscover the joy of coloring outside the lines!

CHAPTER 9

THE ZEN OF COLORING: ADULT COLORING BOOKS FOR STRESS RELIEF AND MINDFULNESS

Remember those carefree childhood days when you could lose yourself for hours in a coloring book? Well, it's time to recapture that joy! Adult coloring books have taken the world by storm, and for good reason. They offer a simple yet powerful way to relax, de-stress, and tap into your creative side. In this chapter, we'll explore how this seemingly simple activity can become a transformative practice for mindfulness and stress relief.

WHY COLORING WORKS WONDERS FOR ADULTS

You might be wondering, "Isn't coloring just for kids?" Not at all! The appeal of adult coloring lies in its ability to engage our minds in a way that's both focused and relaxing. When you're coloring, you're giving your brain a break from the constant chatter of daily worries and to-do lists. Instead, you're concentrating on choosing colors and staying within the lines (or not—we'll get to that!).

This focused attention is a form of meditation. It allows you to enter a state of flow, where you're fully absorbed in the present moment. This can lead to reduced anxiety, improved mood, and even better sleep. Plus, there's the satisfaction of creating something beautiful, even if you don't consider yourself "artistic."

The variety of adult coloring books available is truly astounding. You might find yourself drawn to intricate mandalas, detailed nature scenes, abstract patterns, or even coloring books featuring inspirational quotes or themes from your favorite fandoms. Don't be afraid to try different styles to see what resonates with you. You might be surprised by what you enjoy!

When it comes to coloring tools, you have plenty of options. While you can certainly start with a simple set of colored pencils, part of the fun of adult coloring is experimenting with different mediums. Colored pencils offer precision and blending capabilities, while markers are great for bold, vibrant colors. Gel pens can add sparkle and shine to your creations, and watercolor pencils can be used dry or with water for a paint-like effect. Remember, you don't need to invest in expensive supplies to get started. Begin with what you have or what's comfortable for your budget, and you can always expand your collection as your interest grows.

MINDFULNESS IN EVERY STROKE

Coloring can be more than just a relaxing hobby—it can be a mindfulness practice. Before you begin, take a moment to set an intention for your coloring time. It could be to relax, to boost your mood, or simply to enjoy the process. As you color, pay attention to the feel of the pencil or marker in your hand, the sound it makes on the paper, the scent of the materials. If you find your mind wandering, gently bring your attention back to your breath and the act of coloring.

Don't worry about staying perfectly within the lines or choosing the "right" colors. Allow yourself to be playful and experimental. You might try blending colors in unexpected ways, extending patterns beyond the given design, or adding your own details or doodles to the existing artwork. Remember, there's no "wrong" way to color. This is your time for self-expression and relaxation.

To get the most benefit from adult coloring, try to make it a regular part of your routine. Keep a coloring book and pencils on your nightstand for a relaxing bedtime ritual, or carry a small coloring book in your bag for stress relief on the go. You might schedule a weekly "coloring date" with friends or family, or use coloring as a warm-up for other creative activities or problem-solving tasks.

THE SOCIAL SIDE OF COLORING

While coloring can be a wonderfully solitary activity, it can also be a great way to connect with others. Many communities have adult coloring clubs where you can meet like-minded people and share techniques. You might even consider hosting a coloring party—it's a low-pressure way to socialize and be creative together.

As you explore the world of adult coloring, remember that the true value lies in the process, not the product. It's not about creating a masterpiece (though you might surprise yourself!), but about giving yourself the gift of peaceful, creative time. Embrace imperfection and allow yourself to play with color and form without judgment.

The beauty of adult coloring lies in its accessibility. Unlike some hobbies that require extensive training or expensive equipment, coloring is something you can do anytime, anywhere. Whether you have five minutes or five hours, whether you're at home or on a lunch break at work, you can pick up your coloring book and immerse yourself in a world of color and pattern.

As you continue to explore this relaxing hobby, you may find that it influences other areas of your life. The mindfulness skills you develop through coloring can be applied to other activities, helping you stay present and focused throughout your day. The color combinations you discover might inspire your fashion choices or home decor. And the sense of accomplishment you feel after completing a page can boost your confidence and motivation in other areas.

So grab those colors and let your stress melt away as you bring beautiful designs to life. You might just find that this childhood pastime becomes a valuable tool for adult relaxation and self-expression. The simple act of filling in shapes with color can become a powerful practice for managing stress, boosting creativity, and finding moments of peace in your busy life.

Speaking of bringing designs to life, in our next chapter, we'll take our creative expression into the third dimension. Get ready to roll up your sleeves and dive into the world of clay sculpting. We'll explore how working with this tactile medium can be both therapeutic and empowering. It's time to mold your stress away and shape your own serenity!

CHAPTER 10

SCULPTING YOUR SERENITY: THE THERAPEUTIC BENEFITS OF WORKING WITH CLAY

Have you ever watched a potter at work and marveled at how their hands could transform a lump of clay into a beautiful, functional object? There's something almost magical about the process, isn't there? Well, get ready to experience that magic for yourself! In this chapter, we're diving into the world of clay sculpting and exploring how this hands-on art form can be a powerful tool for stress relief, self-expression, and personal growth.

THE TACTILE JOY OF CLAY

Working with clay is a uniquely tactile experience. Unlike many other art forms, sculpting engages your sense of touch in a profound way. As you knead, shape, and mold the clay, you're not just creating art—you're engaging in a form of sensory therapy. The cool, pliable texture of the clay can be incredibly soothing, almost meditative. Many people find that the simple act of manipulating clay helps them relax and let go of stress.

But clay work isn't just about relaxation. It's also a fantastic outlet for creativity and self-expression. With clay, you have the freedom to create almost anything you can imagine. Whether you're crafting functional pottery, abstract sculptures, or detailed figurines, the possibilities are endless. And the best part? There's no need to aim for perfection. The beauty of clay work often lies in its organic, handmade quality.

GETTING STARTED WITH CLAY

If you're new to clay sculpting, don't worry—it's a very accessible art form. You don't need a pottery wheel or a kiln to get started. Air-dry clay or polymer clay are great options for beginners, as they don't require any special equipment. All you need is the clay itself, a few simple tools (many of which you probably already have in your kitchen), and your imagination.

Start by simply playing with the clay. Roll it into balls, flatten it into discs, try coiling it into spirals. Get a feel for how it responds to your touch. As you become more comfortable, you can start attempting simple projects. Maybe a pinch pot, a small animal figure, or a decorative tile. Remember, the goal isn't to create a masterpiece on your first try. It's about enjoying the process and learning as you go.

THE MINDFULNESS OF MOLDING

One of the most powerful benefits of clay work is how it can help you practice mindfulness. When you're focused on shaping your clay, your mind naturally settles into the present moment. You're not worrying about tomorrow's meeting or replaying yesterday's conversation. You're simply here, now, with the clay in your hands.

This present-moment awareness can be incredibly calming and centering. It's a chance to step away from the constant chatter of your thoughts and immerse yourself in a tactile, creative experience. Many people find that this mindful state carries over into other areas of their lives, helping them stay more grounded and centered even when they're not working with clay.

EXPRESSING EMOTIONS THROUGH CLAY

Clay can also be a powerful medium for emotional expression. Having a bad day? Try pounding and kneading a lump of clay—it's a great way to release tension and frustration. Feeling joyful? That energy might translate into a bright, whimsical sculpture. The malleability of clay makes it an ideal material for giving form to your feelings, even ones that are hard to put into words.

This emotional outlet can be particularly helpful during times of stress or transition. Many therapists use clay work as a tool to help clients process complex emotions or traumatic experiences. Even if you're not working with a therapist, you might find that regular clay sculpting sessions help you understand and manage your emotions more effectively.

THE JOY OF IMPERFECTION

One of the most liberating aspects of clay work is that it teaches us to embrace imperfection. Unlike, say, digital design where you can easily undo a mistake, clay requires us to work with what we've created. That fingerprint you accidentally left? It's now part of the piece's character. That wobble in the vase's rim? It makes your creation unique.

Learning to see beauty in these "imperfections" can be a powerful lesson that extends far beyond your clay sculpting practice. It can help you become more accepting of imperfections in other areas of your life and work, reducing stress and increasing satisfaction.

As you continue to explore clay sculpting, you'll likely find that your skills improve naturally over time. But remember, the true value of this practice isn't in creating perfect objects. It's in the joy of creation, the meditative focus, and the tactile connection to your materials. It's about the process, not just the product.

Whether you're crafting functional pottery, expressive sculptures, or simply enjoying the feel of clay in your hands, you're engaging in a practice that humans have found meaningful for thousands of years. There's something profoundly satisfying about creating tangible objects with your own two hands—especially in our increasingly digital world.

So go ahead, get your hands dirty. Squish that clay, mold it, shape it. Let it be a space where you can play, express yourself, and find a moment of peace in your busy day. You might be surprised at how this simple, earthy medium can help you sculpt not just objects, but a sense of serenity in your life.

And speaking of creating beauty with your hands, in our next chapter we'll explore another art form that brings nature's loveliness into your home. Get ready to dive into the world of floral arranging, where we'll discover how the simple act of arranging flowers can become a meditative practice and a way to bring harmony and beauty into your everyday life. It's time to stop and smell the roses—and then artfully arrange them!

CHAPTER 11

FLORAL ARRANGING: CREATING BEAUTY AND HARMONY WITH FLOWERS

Have you ever paused to admire a beautifully arranged bouquet and felt a sense of calm wash over you? There's something magical about flowers, isn't there? Their colors, shapes, and scents have a unique power to uplift our spirits and bring a touch of nature's beauty into our lives. In this chapter, we're going to explore the art of floral arranging and discover how this creative pursuit can become a source of joy, relaxation, and self-expression.

THE BLOSSOMING ART OF FLORAL DESIGN

Floral arranging is more than just putting flowers in a vase. It's an art form that combines color theory, spatial awareness, and an understanding of natural forms. But don't let that intimidate you! At its heart, floral arranging is about play and personal expression. It's a chance to interact with nature's beauty in a hands-on way, creating something unique and ephemeral.

When you arrange flowers, you're not just creating a decorative object. You're crafting an experience. The arrangement you create will bring color, fragrance, and life into your space. It can set a mood, evoke memories, or simply provide a focal point of natural beauty in your home or office.

One of the best things about floral arranging is its accessibility. You don't need expensive flowers from a florist to get started. A handful of wildflowers from a meadow, some interesting branches from your backyard, or even a few stems from the grocery store can be transformed into a lovely arrangement with a bit of creativity.

GETTING STARTED: THE BASICS OF BOUQUET BUILDING

Starting your floral arranging journey doesn't require a lot of specialized equipment. A pair of sharp scissors or floral shears, some clean vases of various sizes, and perhaps some floral foam or a flower frog (a device used to hold stems in place) are all you really need to begin.

When you're ready to create your first arrangement, start by selecting your flowers and foliage. Try to choose a variety of shapes, sizes, and textures. You might want to pick a focal flower - something large and eye-catching - and then select smaller flowers and greenery to complement it.

As you begin to arrange, think about the overall shape you want to create. Classic arrangements often follow a triangular or domed shape, but feel free to experiment with what looks pleasing to your eye. Start with your larger, sturdier stems to create a framework, then fill in with smaller flowers and foliage.

Remember, there's no "right" or "wrong" way to arrange flowers. What matters is that the end result brings you joy. Don't be afraid to play around, try different combinations, and see what speaks to you.

THE MINDFULNESS OF FLORAL ARRANGING

One of the most beautiful aspects of floral arranging is how it can become a mindfulness practice. As you work with your flowers, you naturally become focused on the present moment. You're noticing the subtle variations in color and form, feeling the textures of stems and petals, inhaling the fragrances.

This present-moment awareness can be incredibly calming and centering. It's a chance to step away from the stress and rush of daily life and immerse yourself in a world of natural beauty. Many people find that the peaceful state of mind they achieve while arranging flowers carries over into other areas of their lives.

EXPRESSING YOURSELF THROUGH FLOWERS

Just as a painter uses color and form to express emotions and ideas, you can use flowers to express yourself. Are you feeling bold and energetic? Perhaps a vibrant arrangement of sunflowers and dahlias would reflect that. Seeking calm and serenity? A soft bouquet of white roses and lavender might be just the thing.

You can also use floral arranging to connect with the changing seasons. In spring, you might create arrangements featuring delicate blossoms and fresh green leaves. Summer could bring bold, bright flowers, while autumn might inspire you to work with rich, warm colors and interesting seed pods or berries.

THE JOY OF IMPERMANENCE

One of the unique aspects of floral arranging is its ephemeral nature. Unlike a painting or sculpture that can last for years, a flower arrangement is a temporary creation. While this might seem sad at first, many people find it liberating. It's a reminder to appreciate beauty in the moment, without trying to hold onto it forever.

This concept of impermanence can be a powerful life lesson. It encourages us to fully appreciate the present moment and to find beauty in change and transition. As you watch your arrangements evolve over days, with some flowers fading while others come into full bloom, you're witnessing a beautiful metaphor for life itself.

As you continue to explore the world of floral arranging, you'll likely find that your skills and confidence grow naturally over time. You might start noticing interesting plants and flowers everywhere you go, imagining how you could incorporate them into your next creation. You might find yourself experimenting with unusual containers or combining flowers with other natural elements like stones or driftwood.

Remember, the goal isn't to create perfect, professional-looking arrangements (unless that's what brings you joy!). It's about the process of creating, the pleasure of working with nature's beauty, and the satisfaction of bringing a touch of that beauty into your daily life.

So go ahead, gather some flowers and let your creativity bloom. Whether you're crafting an elaborate centerpiece or simply placing a single perfect bloom in a bud vase, you're engaging in an art form that has brought joy and beauty to human lives for centuries.

And speaking of bringing creativity into your daily life, in our next chapter we'll explore another art form that's both expressive and practical. Get ready to step into the kitchen and discover the "Culinary Canvas" approach to cooking and baking. We'll learn how these everyday activities can become a delicious outlet for your creativity and a source of joy and satisfaction. It's time to whip up some edible art!

CHAPTER 12

THE "CULINARY CANVAS" APPROACH: COOKING AND BAKING AS CREATIVE OUTLETS

Have you ever considered that your kitchen could be your next art studio? Welcome to the delicious world of culinary creativity! In this chapter, we're going to explore how cooking and baking can become more than just daily chores—they can be vibrant, satisfying outlets for your creativity and self-expression.

THE ART OF EDIBLE EXPRESSION

Cooking and baking are often seen as practical skills, necessary for sustenance. But when you approach them with a creative mindset, they transform into something much more exciting. Think of your ingredients as your paints, your pots and pans as your brushes, and your plate as your canvas. Suddenly, meal preparation becomes an opportunity for artistic expression.

This "Culinary Canvas" approach isn't about becoming a professional chef or creating Instagram-worthy dishes (though if that happens, great!). It's about finding joy in the process of creating something delicious and beautiful, even if it's just for yourself or your loved ones.

EMBRACING CULINARY CREATIVITY

So how do you start seeing your kitchen as a creative space? Begin by giving yourself permission to play. Don't be afraid to experiment with flavors, textures, and presentations. Maybe you'll combine spices in a new way, or try plating your usual dinner in a more artistic manner. The goal is to approach cooking with curiosity and a sense of adventure.

Remember, some of the world's most beloved dishes were created by happy accidents or bold experiments. The chocolate chip cookie, for instance, was invented when Ruth Wakefield ran out of baker's chocolate and decided to chop up a semi-sweet chocolate bar instead. Her "mistake" turned into a classic treat loved by millions!

THE MINDFULNESS OF MIXING AND MEASURING

One of the beautiful things about cooking and baking is how they naturally lend themselves to mindfulness. When you're focused on chopping vegetables, kneading dough, or carefully measuring ingredients, you're fully present in the moment. The scents, textures, and sounds of cooking engage all your senses, grounding you in the here and now.

This mindful state can be incredibly relaxing and stress-relieving. Many people find that time spent in the kitchen becomes a form of moving meditation, allowing them to unwind after a long day and transition into a more peaceful state of mind.

EXPRESSING EMOTIONS THROUGH FOOD

Just as other art forms can be outlets for emotional expression, so too can cooking. Having a tough day? Kneading bread dough can be a great way to work out frustrations. Feeling nostalgic? Try recreating a beloved family recipe. Bursting with joy? That might translate into a colorful, celebratory cake or a bright, zesty salad.

Food has a unique power to evoke memories and emotions. By consciously connecting your cooking to your emotional state, you can create dishes that not only nourish your body but also feed your soul.

THE JOY OF IMPERFECTION IN THE KITCHEN

One of the most liberating aspects of approaching cooking creatively is embracing imperfection. Not every dish will turn out exactly as you envision it—and that's okay! Even professional chefs have kitchen failures. The key is to see these "mistakes" as learning opportunities and sometimes even as paths to new discoveries.

Did your cake fall flat? Maybe it can be repurposed into a delicious trifle. Did your experimental spice blend not quite work out? That's valuable information for your next attempt. By embracing the unpredictable nature of cooking, you free yourself to be more adventurous and creative in the kitchen.

As you continue to explore your culinary creativity, you might find yourself looking at recipes in a new way. Instead of following them to the letter, you might start seeing them as springboards for your own ideas. You might begin to understand the principles behind why certain flavors work well together, allowing you to create your own unique combinations.

Remember, the goal of the "Culinary Canvas" approach isn't to become a master chef (unless that's what you want!). It's about finding joy in the process of creation, nourishing yourself and others, and expressing your creativity in a deliciously tangible way.

So tie on that apron and let your culinary creativity flow! Whether you're whipping up a quick weeknight dinner or spending a leisurely Sunday baking, approach it with the eye of an artist. Play with colors, textures, and flavors. Present your dishes with flair. And most importantly, savor the satisfaction of creating something uniquely your own.

As we wrap up our exploration of creative pursuits, it's time to shift gears and get our bodies moving. In the next part of our journey, we'll dive into active hobbies that engage both mind and body. Get ready to discover how physical activities can become powerful tools for boosting your mood, building confidence, and finding your own unique form of moving meditation. It's time to unleash your inner athlete and dancer!

PART III

ACTIVE HOBBIES FOR MIND AND BODY

Welcome to Part III of our journey into empowering pursuits! We've explored the world of creative expression through art, writing, and crafts. Now, it's time to get our bodies moving and discover the incredible benefits of active hobbies. In this section, we'll dive into a variety of physical activities that not only boost your fitness but also nourish your mind and spirit.

THE POWER OF ACTIVE PURSUITS

Have you ever noticed how a brisk walk can clear your head, or how accomplished you feel after a good workout? That's just a taste of what active hobbies can do for you. Physical activities have an incredible power to transform not just our bodies, but our minds and emotions as well.

When we engage in active pursuits, we're not just burning calories or building muscle. We're releasing endorphins, those feel-good chemicals that boost our mood and reduce stress. We're challenging ourselves, building confidence, and developing a stronger connection between our minds and bodies. And often, we're creating opportunities for social connection, whether it's through team sports, group fitness classes, or outdoor adventures with friends.

FINDING YOUR PERFECT FIT

One of the beautiful things about active hobbies is the sheer variety available. Whether you're drawn to the graceful movements of dance, the thrill of adventure sports, the inner strength developed through martial arts, or the peace found in yoga and tai chi, there's an active pursuit out there that's perfect for you.

In the chapters ahead, we'll explore a range of activities, from high-energy workouts to more meditative practices. We'll look at how each of these pursuits can benefit your physical health, mental wellbeing, and overall quality of life. And we'll provide practical tips for getting started, even if you've never considered yourself the "athletic type."

OVERCOMING BARRIERS

For some of us, the idea of taking up an active hobby can be intimidating. Maybe you've had negative experiences with sports in the past, or you're worried about not being fit enough or coordinated enough. Perhaps you're concerned about finding the time or energy for a new physical activity in your busy life.

Rest assured, we'll address these common concerns and provide strategies for overcoming them. Remember, the goal here isn't to become a professional athlete or to transform your body overnight. It's about finding joy in movement, challenging yourself in new ways, and discovering the incredible benefits that active hobbies can bring to your life.

THE JOURNEY AHEAD

As we explore these active pursuits, keep an open mind. You might be surprised by which activities resonate with you. The dance skeptic might find herself falling in love with salsa, while the yoga novice could discover an unexpected passion for rock climbing.

Each chapter will provide an introduction to a different active hobby, along with insights into its benefits, tips for getting started, and inspiration to keep you motivated. We'll also explore how these physical pursuits can complement the creative hobbies we discussed in earlier chapters, creating a well-rounded approach to personal growth and fulfillment.

So lace up your sneakers, roll out your yoga mat, or slip on your dancing shoes. It's time to discover the transformative power of active hobbies and unleash your inner athlete. Let's get moving!

CHAPTER 13

THE "ENDORPHIN EFFECT" OF EXERCISE HOBBIES: BOOSTING MOOD AND CONFIDENCE

Have you ever experienced that amazing post-workout high? That feeling of accomplishment, energy, and overall well-being that comes after a good sweat session? Welcome to the wonderful world of the "Endorphin Effect"! In this chapter, we're going to explore how exercise hobbies can be powerful tools for boosting your mood, building confidence, and transforming your overall sense of self.

UNDERSTANDING THE ENDORPHIN EFFECT

Let's start with a bit of science. When you exercise, your body releases chemicals called endorphins. These natural mood-boosters are often referred to as the body's own "feel-good" drugs. They can reduce pain perception, alleviate stress, and even create a sense of euphoria - that's where the term "runner's high" comes from!

But the benefits of exercise go far beyond just the immediate endorphin rush. Regular physical activity has been shown to reduce symptoms of anxiety and depression, improve sleep quality, boost self-esteem, and increase overall life satisfaction. It's like a wonder drug, but without any of the side effects!

FINDING YOUR EXERCISE GROOVE

Now, before you start groaning at the thought of endless hours on a treadmill, remember this: exercise doesn't have to be a chore. The key is to find activities that you genuinely enjoy. Maybe you love the rhythm and energy of dance classes. Perhaps you find peace and challenge in yoga. Or you might get a thrill from the competition of team sports.

The options are endless, and there's no one-size-fits-all approach. The best exercise hobby for you is the one that you'll stick with. So don't be afraid to experiment until you find your groove. And remember, it's perfectly okay to have multiple exercise hobbies. Variety can keep things interesting and work different aspects of your fitness.

BUILDING CONFIDENCE THROUGH CHALLENGE

One of the most powerful aspects of exercise hobbies is their ability to build confidence. Each time you master a new yoga pose, run a little further, or lift a heavier weight, you're proving to yourself that you're capable of growth and improvement. This sense of accomplishment can spill over into other areas of your life, boosting your overall self-esteem.

Start small and set achievable goals. Maybe it's doing a 5-minute workout every day for a week, or learning the basic steps of a new dance style. As you reach these milestones, celebrate your progress and then set new challenges for yourself. Remember, the journey is just as important as the destination.

THE SOCIAL SIDE OF SWEAT

Exercise hobbies can also be a great way to connect with others. Joining a running club, attending group fitness classes, or being part of a sports team can provide a sense of community and support. These social connections not only make exercise more enjoyable but can also contribute to improved mental health and overall life satisfaction.

Don't worry if you're naturally introverted or feel self-conscious about exercising in front of others. There are plenty of exercise hobbies you can enjoy solo, or you can start by working out with just one trusted friend. The important thing is to find what works for you.

OVERCOMING OBSTACLES

Let's be real: starting a new exercise hobby isn't always easy. You might face challenges like lack of time, low energy, or self-doubt. The key is to anticipate these obstacles and have strategies in place to overcome them.

If time is an issue, try breaking your exercise into shorter, more manageable chunks throughout the day. Feeling low on energy? Remember that exercise often boosts energy levels - you might feel tired at first, but you'll likely feel more energized afterward. And if self-doubt is holding you back, remind yourself that everyone starts somewhere. Focus on your own progress rather than comparing yourself to others.

THE MIND–BODY CONNECTION

As you delve into your chosen exercise hobby, pay attention to how it affects not just your body, but your mind as well. Notice how your mood shifts after a workout, how your stress levels decrease, or how you sleep better at night. This awareness can help motivate you to keep going, even on days when you don't feel like exercising.

You might even find that your exercise hobby becomes a form of moving meditation. Whether you're focusing on your breath during yoga, finding your rhythm in a dance class, or getting into the zone during a long run, these activities can provide a mental break from daily stresses and help you stay present in the moment.

Remember, the goal of embracing an exercise hobby isn't about achieving a certain body type or meeting someone else's standards. It's about feeling good, boosting your mood, and building confidence in your own abilities. So lace up those sneakers, roll out that yoga mat, or hit the dance floor. Your body - and your mind - will thank you for it.

As we continue our exploration of active hobbies, we'll next dive into the joyful world of dance. From ballroom to hip-hop and everything in between, we'll discover how moving to the rhythm can become a powerful form of self-expression and a path to happiness. Get ready to let loose and find your groove!

CHAPTER 14

DANCING YOUR WAY TO HAPPINESS: FROM BALLROOM TO HIP-HOP AND BEYOND

Have you ever found yourself swaying to a catchy tune or tapping your foot to a rhythm without even realizing it? That's your body's natural response to music, and it's the foundation of one of the most joyful forms of exercise: dance. In this chapter, we're going to explore how dancing can become more than just a fun activity—it can be a pathway to happiness, self-expression, and improved physical and mental well-being.

THE UNIVERSAL LANGUAGE OF DANCE

Dance is often called the universal language, and for good reason. It transcends cultural barriers, allows us to express emotions without words, and connects us to our bodies in a unique way. Whether you're gliding across a ballroom floor, grooving to hip-hop beats, or swaying to the gentle rhythms of a slow dance, you're participating in an art form that's as old as humanity itself.

But dance is more than just an art—it's also an incredible form of exercise. It improves cardiovascular health, builds strength and flexibility, enhances coordination, and can even boost cognitive function. And the best part? It's so much fun that you might not even realize you're working out!

One of the beautiful things about dance is the sheer variety of styles available. From elegant ballroom waltzes to energetic hip-hop routines, graceful ballet to passionate salsa, there's a dance style out there for everyone. Each genre offers its own unique benefits and challenges, and many dancers enjoy exploring multiple styles. Don't feel like you have to stick to just one—part of the joy of dance is discovering new ways to move your body and express yourself.

GETTING STARTED: FROM TWO LEFT FEET TO DANCING QUEEN

If you're new to dance, the idea of stepping onto a dance floor might feel intimidating. But remember, everyone starts as a beginner. The key is to start with classes or tutorials designed for absolute beginners. Many dance studios offer introductory courses that break down basic steps and rhythms in a supportive environment.

As you begin your dance journey, try not to worry about looking perfect. Instead, focus on feeling the music and enjoying the movement. Wear comfortable clothing that allows you to move freely, and be patient with yourself. Learning to dance takes time, but the journey is half the fun!

Consider starting with a friend for moral support, or embrace the opportunity to meet new people in class. Dance is inherently social, and you might find that the shared experience of learning something new helps you connect with others in a comfortable, low-pressure way.

THE EMOTIONAL BENEFITS OF DANCE

Beyond the physical benefits, dance can have a profound impact on your emotional well-being. It's a powerful stress-reliever, helping to reduce tension and anxiety. The combination of music, movement, and often social interaction can boost your mood and increase feelings of happiness.

Dance can also be a form of emotional expression. Having a bad day? Let it out through a high-energy routine. Feeling joyful? Express it through exuberant movements. Dance allows us to communicate and process emotions in a unique, physical way.

As you progress in your dance journey, you'll likely notice an increase in confidence. Learning new steps, mastering routines, and perhaps even performing for others can boost your self-esteem in powerful ways. This newfound confidence often spills over into other areas of life, from work to personal relationships.

DANCE AS MINDFULNESS PRACTICE

When you're fully engaged in dance, you're practicing a form of mindfulness. You're focused on the present moment—the music, your body's movements, your partner or the other dancers around you. This present-moment awareness can be incredibly calming and centering, providing a break from the stresses and worries of daily life.

Even if you're naturally introverted, you might find that dance provides a comfortable way to interact with others. The shared focus on learning and enjoying movement can take the pressure off social interactions. Many people find that dance classes or social dance events become a cherished part of their routine, offering both exercise and community.

Don't be discouraged if you feel awkward or uncoordinated at first. Every dancer, even the professionals, started as a beginner. Embrace the learning process and celebrate your improvements, no matter how small they might seem. Each time you master a new step or routine, you're proving to yourself that you're capable of growth and learning.

As you continue to explore the world of dance, remember that it's not about perfection. It's about joy, self-expression, and the simple pleasure of moving your body to music. Whether you dream of competing in ballroom competitions or just want to feel more comfortable on the dance floor at weddings, dance has something to offer everyone.

The beauty of dance as a hobby is its accessibility. You don't need expensive equipment or a specific location to practice. With just a bit of space and some music, you can dance anywhere—in your living room, at the park, or even while doing chores around the house. It's a hobby that can easily fit into your lifestyle, bringing moments of joy and movement to your everyday routine.

So put on your favorite tunes, clear some space, and let your body move. You might just dance your way to a happier, healthier you! Whether you're swaying to a slow song, shaking it to some pop hits, or trying out some salsa steps, remember that every movement is a celebration of music, your body, and life itself.

Speaking of getting your body moving in exciting ways, our next chapter will dive into the world of adventure sports. From rock climbing to surfing, we'll explore how these thrilling activities can push your limits, build confidence, and connect you with nature in powerful ways. Get ready for an adrenaline rush as we take our pursuit of active hobbies to new heights—literally!

CHAPTER 15

THE THRILL OF ADVENTURE SPORTS: EMPOWERMENT THROUGH ROCK CLIMBING, SURFING, AND MORE

Have you ever dreamed of scaling a sheer rock face, riding the perfect wave, or soaring through the air on a zip line? Welcome to the exhilarating world of adventure sports! In this chapter, we'll explore how these heart-pumping activities can not only give you an adrenaline rush but also boost your confidence, connect you with nature, and push your limits in the most empowering ways.

EMBRACING THE ADVENTURE MINDSET

Adventure sports are about more than just physical prowess. They're about cultivating a mindset of courage, resilience, and openness to new experiences. When you step out of your comfort zone to try something like rock climbing or surfing, you're not just challenging your body - you're expanding your sense of what's possible.

These activities often require us to face our fears head-on. Maybe it's the fear of heights as you look up at a climbing route, or the intimidation of powerful waves as you paddle out on a surfboard. But here's the secret: each time you confront these fears and push through them, you're building mental strength that carries over into every aspect of your life.

ROCK CLIMBING: SCALING NEW HEIGHTS

Let's start with rock climbing, an sport that's surged in popularity in recent years. Whether you're scaling an indoor wall or tackling outdoor cliffs, climbing offers a unique combination of physical challenge and problem-solving. It's like a vertical puzzle, requiring strength, flexibility, and strategic thinking.

One of the beautiful things about climbing is how it forces you to stay present. When you're on the wall, your focus narrows to the next hold, the next move. All the worries and stresses of daily life fade away, replaced by an intense concentration on the here and now.

Climbing also teaches us valuable lessons about perseverance. You might not make it to the top on your first try - or your second, or your tenth. But each attempt teaches you something new about the route and about yourself. The satisfaction of finally conquering a challenging climb is hard to beat.

SURFING: DANCING WITH THE WAVES

Now, let's shift from vertical challenges to horizontal ones. Surfing is often described as a spiritual experience as much as a physical one. There's something magical about being out on the water, feeling the power of the ocean beneath you, and working in harmony with nature to catch that perfect wave.

Like climbing, surfing requires a blend of physical skill and mental focus. It teaches patience as you wait for the right wave, resilience as you wipe out and get back on the board, and respect for the power of nature. Many surfers describe feeling a profound sense of peace and connection to the world around them when they're out on the water.

OTHER THRILLING OPTIONS

While we've focused on climbing and surfing, the world of adventure sports is vast and varied. You might find your thrill in mountain biking, conquering rugged trails and feeling the rush of wind in your face. Or perhaps you're drawn to the freefall of skydiving, experiencing the ultimate leap of faith.

Whitewater rafting offers the excitement of navigating rushing rivers, working as a team to conquer rapids. Zip lining lets you soar through forest canopies, offering a bird's eye view of nature. The key is to explore and find the adventure sport that resonates with you.

BUILDING CONFIDENCE THROUGH CHALLENGE

One of the most powerful benefits of adventure sports is the boost they give to your self-confidence. Each time you accomplish something you once thought impossible - whether it's reaching the top of a climb or standing up on a surfboard - you're proving to yourself that you're capable of amazing things.

This confidence isn't limited to the sport itself. The courage and resilience you develop through adventure sports often spill over into other areas of life. You might find yourself more willing to take on challenges at work, or more confident in social situations.

CONNECTING WITH NATURE AND COMMUNITY

Adventure sports offer a unique way to connect with the natural world. Whether you're scaling a cliff face, riding ocean waves, or hiking to a mountain summit, you're immersing yourself in nature in a visceral, hands-on way. This connection can foster a deep appreciation for the environment and a desire to protect it.

These sports also often come with vibrant communities. Climbers, surfers, and other adventure enthusiasts tend to be passionate, supportive groups. You might find that your new hobby comes with a built-in social circle, united by a shared love for the sport and the outdoors.

SAFETY FIRST

It's important to note that while adventure sports are thrilling, they do come with risks. Always prioritize safety by taking lessons from qualified instructors, using proper equipment, and respecting your limits. Remember, the goal is to challenge yourself, not endanger yourself.

As you explore the world of adventure sports, remember that it's not about being the fastest, strongest, or most daring. It's about pushing your own limits, connecting with nature, and discovering new aspects of yourself. Whether you're hanging from a cliff or paddling into a wave, you're embarking on a journey of self-discovery and empowerment.

So, are you ready to take the leap into adventure sports? Whether you choose to start small with an indoor climbing wall or dive right into surfing lessons, you're opening the door to a world of excitement, challenge, and personal growth.

Speaking of personal growth and empowerment, our next chapter will explore another type of adventurous pursuit - the world of martial arts. We'll discover how these ancient practices can build physical strength, mental discipline, and inner peace. Get ready to bow onto the mat and embark on a journey of self-discovery through the art of combat!

CHAPTER 16

MARTIAL ARTS MASTERY: BUILDING STRENGTH, DISCIPLINE, AND INNER PEACE

Have you ever watched a martial arts demonstration and marveled at the blend of power, grace, and focus on display? Welcome to the world of martial arts, where ancient traditions meet modern fitness, and where physical prowess intertwines with mental discipline. In this chapter, we'll explore how practicing martial arts can not only strengthen your body but also cultivate inner peace and transform your approach to life's challenges.

THE PATH OF THE WARRIOR

Martial arts encompass a wide range of fighting styles and traditions, each with its own unique philosophy and techniques. From the flowing movements of Tai Chi to the powerful strikes of Karate, the grappling techniques of Judo to the strategic mind games of Brazilian Jiu-Jitsu, there's a martial art out there for everyone.

But martial arts are about much more than just learning to fight. They're about developing self-discipline, respect for others, and a deep understanding of your own capabilities. Many practitioners find that the lessons learned on the mat or in the dojo translate directly to other areas of their lives, helping them navigate challenges with grace and confidence.

PHYSICAL BENEFITS: MORE THAN JUST SELF-DEFENSE

Let's start with the obvious: martial arts are an incredible workout. Regular practice can improve your strength, flexibility, balance, and cardiovascular fitness. You'll develop better coordination and body awareness as you learn to execute complex movements and techniques.

But the physical benefits go beyond just fitness. Martial arts can improve your posture, reduce chronic pain, and enhance your overall body mechanics. The focus on proper form and controlled movements can help prevent injuries in daily life. And of course, you'll be learning valuable self-defense skills along the way.

MENTAL DISCIPLINE AND EMOTIONAL BALANCE

Perhaps even more profound than the physical benefits are the mental and emotional transformations that often occur through martial arts practice. The intense focus required to master complex techniques can improve your concentration and mental clarity. Many practitioners report reduced stress and anxiety, better emotional regulation, and increased self-confidence.

Martial arts also teach valuable lessons in perseverance and humility. You'll face challenges and setbacks as you progress, learning to pick yourself up after a fall (sometimes literally) and keep pushing forward. This resilience can be a powerful asset in all areas of life.

Many martial arts are deeply rooted in Eastern philosophies, emphasizing concepts like mindfulness, respect, and the balance of opposing forces. For example, the concept of "yin and yang" in Chinese martial arts teaches the importance of balance and harmony. The Japanese concept of "zanshin" in sword arts emphasizes constant awareness and readiness.

As you delve deeper into your chosen martial art, you may find yourself absorbing these philosophical principles and applying them to your daily life. Many practitioners find that martial arts become not just a physical practice, but a way of life.

CHOOSING YOUR PATH

With so many martial arts to choose from, how do you decide where to start? Here are a few popular options to consider:

- Karate: Known for its powerful striking techniques and emphasis on discipline.
- Taekwondo: Features high, fast kicks and a strong Olympic sport presence.
- Judo: Focuses on throws and grappling, great for learning how to use an opponent's energy against them.
- Brazilian Jiu-Jitsu: Emphasizes ground fighting and submission techniques.
- Tai Chi: A slower-paced, meditative practice that's excellent for improving balance and reducing stress.

Remember, the best martial art for you is one that you enjoy and can commit to practicing regularly. Many schools offer trial classes, so don't be afraid to try a few different styles before settling on one.

GETTING STARTED: FROM WHITE BELT TO WARRIOR

Starting a martial arts practice can feel intimidating, but remember: every black belt was once a beginner. Look for a reputable school or dojo in your area with qualified instructors. Most martial arts schools welcome beginners of all ages and fitness levels.

As you begin your journey, focus on learning proper form and technique rather than trying to progress quickly. Martial arts is about the journey, not the destination. Embrace the beginner's mindset, stay open to feedback, and don't be afraid to make mistakes—that's how you'll grow.

One often overlooked benefit of martial arts is the sense of community it can provide. Training alongside others, supporting each other's progress, and sharing in the challenges and triumphs can create strong bonds. Many practitioners find that their dojo becomes a second family, offering support and encouragement both on and off the mat.

As you progress in your martial arts journey, you'll likely find that the benefits extend far beyond the physical. You may discover a new sense of calm in stressful situations, improved focus at work or school, and a deeper understanding of yourself and your capabilities. The discipline, respect, and perseverance you cultivate in your practice can become powerful tools for navigating life's challenges.

So, are you ready to bow onto the mat and begin your martial arts journey? Whether you're drawn to the graceful movements of Tai Chi or the intense grappling of Brazilian Jiu-Jitsu, you're embarking on a path of physical, mental, and spiritual growth. Remember, the goal isn't to become a fearsome fighter, but to become the best version of yourself.

As we move from the disciplined world of martial arts, our next chapter will take us into the nurturing embrace of nature. We'll explore the "Green Thumb Glow" of gardening, discovering how cultivating plants can bring joy, serenity, and a deep connection to the natural world. Get ready to dig in and watch your garden—and your sense of well-being—bloom!

CHAPTER 17

THE "GREEN THUMB GLOW" OF GARDENING: CULTIVATING JOY AND SERENITY IN NATURE

Have you ever noticed how a walk in a lush garden can instantly lift your spirits? There's something magical about being surrounded by growing things, isn't there? Welcome to the world of gardening, where you can create your own little piece of paradise and nurture both plants and your own well-being. In this chapter, we'll explore how getting your hands dirty can lead to a clearer mind, a happier heart, and a deeper connection with nature.

SOWING THE SEEDS OF SERENITY

Gardening is more than just a hobby - it's a form of therapy that's been recognized for its powerful effects on mental health. The act of tending to plants, whether it's a sprawling backyard garden or a few pots on your windowsill, can reduce stress, anxiety, and symptoms of depression. There's something profoundly soothing about the rhythmic nature of gardening tasks, from digging and planting to watering and pruning.

But the benefits don't stop there. Gardening also provides a sense of purpose and accomplishment. Watching a seed you've planted grow into a flourishing plant can be incredibly rewarding. It's a tangible reminder of your ability to nurture and create, which can boost self-esteem and provide a sense of empowerment.

THE PHYSICAL PERKS OF PLAYING IN THE DIRT

While gardening might not seem like an intense workout, it's actually a great form of low-impact exercise. Digging, planting, weeding, and other gardening activities can improve strength, flexibility, and cardiovascular health. Plus, spending time outdoors in the sunlight helps your body produce vitamin D, essential for strong bones and a healthy immune system.

There's also growing evidence that getting your hands in the soil can have surprising health benefits. Exposure to certain bacteria in soil has been linked to increased serotonin production in the brain, potentially improving mood and cognitive function. It seems that "grounding" yourself through gardening isn't just a metaphor - it can have real physiological effects!

CULTIVATING MINDFULNESS IN THE GARDEN

Gardening naturally lends itself to mindfulness practice. As you work with plants, you're encouraged to be present in the moment, noticing the texture of the soil, the scent of the flowers, the sound of rustling leaves. This sensory engagement can help quiet the mind and bring a sense of peace and centeredness.

Moreover, gardening teaches patience and acceptance. Plants grow at their own pace, and sometimes despite our best efforts, they don't thrive. Learning to work with nature rather than trying to control it can be a powerful lesson in letting go and accepting the natural flow of life.

GETTING STARTED: FROM BROWN THUMB TO GREEN

If you're new to gardening, don't worry - everyone starts somewhere! Begin with easy-to-grow plants like herbs, succulents, or hardy perennials. Start small with a few pots or a small patch of soil, and gradually expand as you gain confidence and experience.

Remember, gardening is about the journey, not just the destination. Don't be discouraged if your first attempts aren't picture-perfect. Every "failure" is an opportunity to learn and grow (pun intended!). Embrace the process, ask for advice from more experienced gardeners, and most importantly, have fun!

Consider joining a community garden if you don't have space at home. These shared spaces offer not only a place to grow plants but also opportunities to connect with other gardeners, share knowledge, and build community.

THE JOY OF GROWING YOUR OWN FOOD

There's something incredibly satisfying about eating a meal made with vegetables you've grown yourself. Even if it's just a few herbs on your windowsill or a tomato plant on your balcony, growing your own food can give you a new appreciation for where your food comes from and how it's produced.

Vegetable gardening can also encourage healthier eating habits. When you've put time and effort into growing those carrots or lettuce, you're more likely to want to eat them! Plus, nothing beats the flavor of freshly picked produce.

GARDENING FOR THE GREATER GOOD

Your gardening hobby can have positive impacts beyond your own well-being. By creating green spaces, you're contributing to the health of your local ecosystem. Plants absorb carbon dioxide, release oxygen, and provide habitats for beneficial insects and birds.

If you're feeling particularly ambitious, consider planting a pollinator garden to support bees and butterflies, or growing extra vegetables to donate to local food banks. Gardening can be a beautiful way to care for yourself while also caring for your community and the planet.

As you embark on your gardening journey, remember that it's not about creating a perfect, magazine-worthy landscape. It's about connecting with nature, nurturing life, and finding moments of peace and joy in the simple act of helping things grow. Whether you're tending to a vast vegetable plot or lovingly caring for a single potted plant, you're participating in an age-old practice that nourishes both body and soul.

So grab those gardening gloves, pick up a trowel, and get ready to experience the "green thumb glow" for yourself. You might be surprised at how much growth you see - not just in your plants, but in yourself as well.

Speaking of growth and balance, our next chapter will explore another practice that nurtures both body and mind. Get ready to roll out your mat as we dive into the world of yoga and Pilates. We'll discover how these mindful movement practices can help you build strength, flexibility, and inner calm. It's time to breathe deep and find your center!

CHAPTER 18

YOGA AND PILATES: BALANCING MIND, BODY, AND SPIRIT

Have you ever yearned for a way to stretch not just your body, but also your mind and spirit? Welcome to the transformative world of yoga and Pilates. These popular practices offer a unique blend of physical exercise, mental focus, and spiritual growth that can help you find balance in our often chaotic world. In this chapter, we'll explore how these mindful movement practices can strengthen your body, calm your mind, and nourish your soul.

THE ANCIENT WISDOM OF YOGA

Yoga, with its roots in ancient Indian philosophy, is far more than just a series of physical postures. It's a holistic approach to wellbeing that encompasses breath work, meditation, and ethical principles. The word "yoga" itself means "union," referring to the connection of mind, body, and spirit.

At its core, yoga is about finding balance and harmony within yourself and with the world around you. Through a combination of physical postures (asanas), breathing exercises (pranayama), and meditation, yoga helps you develop strength, flexibility, and inner calm. But the benefits go far beyond the physical. Regular yoga practice can reduce stress, improve sleep, boost mood, and even help manage chronic pain conditions.

One of the beautiful things about yoga is its adaptability. There are many different styles, from the gentle, restorative practices of Yin Yoga to the more physically challenging Power Yoga. No matter your age, fitness level, or physical limitations, there's a yoga practice that can work for you.

THE MODERN MAGIC OF PILATES

While yoga has ancient roots, Pilates is a more modern practice, developed in the early 20th century by Joseph Pilates. Originally created as a rehabilitation program for injured soldiers, Pilates has evolved into a popular fitness system that focuses on core strength, flexibility, and body awareness.

Pilates emphasizes controlled movements, proper alignment, and the connection between physical and mental health. The practice is centered around six key principles: concentration, control, center, flow, precision, and breathing. By focusing on these principles, Pilates helps you develop a strong core, improve posture, increase body awareness, and enhance overall strength and flexibility.

Like yoga, Pilates can be adapted to different fitness levels and goals. Whether you're recovering from an injury, looking to improve your athletic performance, or simply wanting to build a stronger, more flexible body, Pilates offers a path to achieve your goals.

MIND-BODY CONNECTION: THE HEART OF BOTH PRACTICES

Both yoga and Pilates emphasize the importance of the mind-body connection. In both practices, you're encouraged to focus your attention on your breath and the sensations in your body as you move. This mindful awareness not only enhances the physical benefits of the exercises but also serves as a form of moving meditation.

This focus on the present moment can have profound effects on mental health. Many practitioners find that regular yoga or Pilates practice helps reduce anxiety, improve concentration, and foster a greater sense of overall wellbeing. The mindfulness skills developed on the mat often translate into daily life, helping you stay calmer and more centered even in stressful situations.

GETTING STARTED: FINDING YOUR PRACTICE

If you're new to yoga or Pilates, the best way to start is with a beginner's class led by a qualified instructor. This ensures that you learn proper form and alignment, reducing the risk of injury. Many gyms and studios offer introductory classes, and there are also numerous online resources for those who prefer to practice at home.

When choosing between yoga and Pilates, consider your goals and what resonates with you. If you're drawn to the spiritual aspects of practice and enjoy a variety of movement styles, yoga might be your best bet. If you're more interested in core strength and precise, controlled movements, Pilates could be the way to go. And remember, there's no rule saying you can't do both!

As you begin your practice, be patient with yourself. Both yoga and Pilates require time and consistency to see results. Focus on how you feel during and after your practice rather than trying to achieve perfect poses or movements. The journey is just as important as the destination.

BEYOND THE MAT: INTEGRATING PRACTICE INTO DAILY LIFE

The true power of yoga and Pilates lies in how they can transform your life off the mat. The body awareness you develop can help you maintain better posture throughout the day. The breathing techniques can be used to manage stress in challenging situations. The mindfulness cultivated in practice can help you stay present and engaged in all aspects of your life.

Many practitioners find that the principles of yoga or Pilates start to influence their lifestyle choices. You might find yourself naturally gravitating towards healthier foods, prioritizing sleep, or seeking out other forms of self-care. This holistic approach to wellness is one of the most profound benefits of these practices.

As you embark on your yoga or Pilates journey, remember that it's not about perfection or comparison. It's about connecting with your body, calming your mind, and nurturing your spirit. Whether you're flowing through a sun salutation or perfecting your Pilates hundred, you're giving yourself the gift of mindful movement and self-care.

So roll out your mat, take a deep breath, and prepare to discover the transformative power of yoga and Pilates. You might just find that these practices become not just a part of your exercise routine, but a way of life.

As we move from the focused practices of yoga and Pilates, our next chapter will introduce you to another ancient form of movement that promotes balance, mindfulness, and inner peace. Get ready to explore the gentle yet powerful world of Tai Chi and Qigong. We'll discover how these meditative practices can enhance your health, reduce stress, and bring a sense of harmony to your daily life. It's time to harness the flow of your inner energy!

CHAPTER 19

THE MEDITATIVE MAGIC OF TAI CHI AND QIGONG: ANCIENT PRACTICES FOR MODERN WOMEN

Have you ever watched a group of people in a park, moving slowly and gracefully in unison, their movements as fluid as water? Chances are, you've witnessed the ancient Chinese practices of Tai Chi or Qigong. In this chapter, we'll explore these gentle yet powerful forms of moving meditation and discover how they can bring balance, health, and serenity to your busy modern life.

UNDERSTANDING TAI CHI AND QIGONG

While often grouped together, Tai Chi and Qigong are distinct practices with some overlapping principles. Tai Chi, originally developed as a martial art, is a series of slow, flowing movements that emphasize balance, flexibility, and internal energy flow. Qigong, which literally means "life energy cultivation," focuses on coordinating breath with simple movements and meditation to enhance the body's natural healing abilities.

Both practices are rooted in Traditional Chinese Medicine and the concept of "qi" (pronounced "chee"), the vital energy that flows through all living things. By practicing these arts, you're said to balance and cultivate your qi, leading to improved health, mental clarity, and overall wellbeing.

THE HEALTH BENEFITS: MORE THAN MEETS THE EYE

Don't let the gentle nature of these practices fool you - they pack a powerful punch when it comes to health benefits. Regular practice of Tai Chi or Qigong has been shown to improve balance and reduce the risk of falls, especially in older adults. They can also enhance flexibility, strengthen muscles (particularly core muscles), and improve cardiovascular health.

But the benefits go far beyond the physical. These practices are known for their stress-reducing effects, helping to lower blood pressure and improve sleep quality. Many practitioners report decreased anxiety and depression, improved mood, and a greater sense of overall wellbeing. Some studies have even suggested that Tai Chi and Qigong can boost immune function and help manage chronic conditions like fibromyalgia and arthritis.

MINDFULNESS IN MOTION

One of the most profound aspects of Tai Chi and Qigong is their ability to cultivate mindfulness. As you perform the slow, deliberate movements, you're encouraged to focus on your breath and the sensations in your body. This present-moment awareness can help quiet the mind and reduce the constant chatter of thoughts that often contribute to stress and anxiety.

This mindfulness aspect makes Tai Chi and Qigong excellent complements to other forms of meditation. Many people find these moving meditations easier to stick with than seated meditation practices, especially if they struggle with sitting still for long periods.

GETTING STARTED: FINDING YOUR FLOW

One of the beautiful things about Tai Chi and Qigong is that they're accessible to almost everyone, regardless of age or fitness level. You don't need any special equipment - just comfortable, loose-fitting clothes and flat shoes (or bare feet).

To begin, look for beginner classes in your area. Many community centers, gyms, and parks offer Tai Chi or Qigong classes. Starting with an instructor is important to ensure you learn proper form and breathing techniques. As you progress, you might choose to supplement your classes with home practice using online videos or apps.

Remember, these are practices of patience and consistency. Don't worry if the movements feel awkward at first or if you can't remember all the steps in a sequence. Focus on the experience of moving and breathing, and let the rest come naturally with time.

INTEGRATING TAI CHI AND QIGONG INTO DAILY LIFE

One of the great things about these practices is that they can be easily integrated into your daily routine. You don't need a full hour - even 5-10 minutes of practice can be beneficial. Try starting your day with a few Qigong exercises to energize your body and focus your mind. Or use Tai Chi movements as a midday break to reset and de-stress.

Many of the principles of Tai Chi and Qigong can be applied to everyday activities. The focus on proper posture and alignment can help improve your posture throughout the day. The emphasis on smooth, controlled breathing can be a valuable tool for managing stress in challenging situations.

As you explore Tai Chi and Qigong, you might find that they influence other aspects of your life. Many practitioners report developing a greater sense of patience, both with themselves and others. You might notice improved body awareness that carries over into other physical activities. Some people even find that the flowing, circular movements of these practices inspire a more flexible, adaptable approach to life's challenges.

Remember, there's no "perfect" way to practice Tai Chi or Qigong. The goal is not to achieve a flawless performance, but to cultivate a sense of harmony between your body, mind, and breath. Embrace the journey of learning and discovery, and allow yourself to be fully present in each moment of practice.

So why not give Tai Chi or Qigong a try? You might just find that these ancient practices offer exactly the balance and serenity you've been seeking in your modern life. As you cultivate your inner energy and find your flow, you may discover a new sense of calm and centeredness that extends far beyond your practice sessions.

Speaking of finding balance and connecting with nature, our next chapter will take us out of the studio and into the great outdoors. Get ready to lace up your hiking boots as we explore the empowering world of hiking and backpacking. We'll discover how venturing into nature can not only improve your physical fitness but also boost your confidence, clear your mind, and provide a profound sense of connection to the world around you. It's time to hit the trail and discover the transformative power of the great outdoors!

CHAPTER 20

HIKING AND BACKPACKING: DISCOVERING EMPOWERMENT IN THE GREAT OUTDOORS

Have you ever felt the thrill of reaching a mountain summit, or the peace that comes from walking through a sun-dappled forest? Welcome to the world of hiking and backpacking, where every step can lead to adventure, self-discovery, and a profound connection with nature. In this chapter, we'll explore how hitting the trails can not only improve your physical fitness but also boost your confidence, clear your mind, and provide a deep sense of empowerment.

THE CALL OF THE WILD

There's something primal about venturing into nature, away from the hustle and bustle of modern life. Hiking and backpacking offer a unique opportunity to disconnect from technology and reconnect with the natural world. As you walk among trees, beside streams, or up mountain paths, you're not just exercising your body - you're nourishing your soul.

The benefits of hiking go far beyond physical fitness. Studies have shown that spending time in nature can reduce stress, improve mood, and even boost cognitive function. The combination of physical activity, fresh air, and natural surroundings creates a powerful tonic for both mind and body.

BUILDING STRENGTH AND ENDURANCE

Don't underestimate the physical challenge of hiking. Whether you're tackling a gentle nature trail or a steep mountain path, you're engaging multiple muscle groups and improving your cardiovascular health. Hiking can help build leg strength, core stability, and overall endurance. And the best part? It rarely feels like a workout because you're too busy enjoying the scenery and the journey.

Backpacking takes these physical benefits a step further. Carrying a pack with supplies for overnight or multi-day trips adds an extra strength-building element to your hike. It also teaches valuable skills in efficiency and minimalism - you quickly learn what's essential and what's not when you have to carry everything on your back!

EMPOWERMENT THROUGH CHALLENGE

One of the most powerful aspects of hiking and backpacking is the sense of achievement they provide. There's nothing quite like the feeling of reaching a summit you've been climbing for hours, or completing a challenging trail you weren't sure you could manage. These accomplishments build confidence that often spills over into other areas of life.

Hiking also teaches valuable life skills like problem-solving, risk assessment, and self-reliance. When you're out on the trail, you need to be prepared for changing weather, navigate your route, and sometimes make quick decisions. These experiences can make you feel more capable and confident in your daily life.

MINDFULNESS ON THE TRAIL

Hiking naturally lends itself to mindfulness. As you walk, you become acutely aware of your surroundings - the feel of the ground beneath your feet, the sound of birds or rustling leaves, the scent of pine or wildflowers. This sensory engagement can help quiet the mind and bring you into the present moment.

Many hikers describe experiencing a meditative state on long hikes, where the rhythm of walking and breathing creates a sense of flow. This can be incredibly calming and centering, providing a break from the constant mental chatter of daily life.

GETTING STARTED: FROM DAY HIKES TO BACKCOUNTRY ADVENTURES

If you're new to hiking, start small. Look for local nature trails or easy day hikes in your area. As you build confidence and fitness, you can gradually tackle longer and more challenging trails. Many state and national parks offer a range of hiking options for different skill levels.

For those interested in backpacking, consider taking a class or joining a group for your first overnight trip. You'll learn essential skills like how to pack efficiently, set up camp, and practice Leave No Trace principles to protect the environment.

Remember to always prioritize safety. Let someone know your hiking plans, carry essentials like water, snacks, and a first aid kit, and be prepared for changing weather conditions. Many hiking apps and websites provide trail information and maps to help you plan your adventures.

CONNECTING WITH NATURE AND COMMUNITY

Hiking and backpacking offer unique opportunities to connect with nature in a profound way. As you spend more time outdoors, you may find yourself developing a deeper appreciation for the natural world and a stronger desire to protect it.

These activities can also be wonderfully social. Joining a hiking club or going on group backpacking trips can help you meet like-minded people and form lasting friendships. There's something special about sharing the challenge of a difficult hike or the beauty of a spectacular view with others.

As you embark on your hiking and backpacking adventures, remember that it's not about covering the most miles or climbing the highest peaks. It's about the journey, the moments of beauty and challenge along the way, and the personal growth that comes from pushing your boundaries.

So lace up those hiking boots, pack your backpack, and step out onto the trail. Whether you're exploring a local park or venturing into the backcountry, you're embarking on a journey of empowerment, self-discovery, and connection with the natural world. Who knows what you might discover about yourself and the world around you with each step you take?

As we conclude our exploration of active hobbies, we've journeyed through various ways to engage our bodies and minds. In the next part of our book, we'll shift gears to explore intellectual pursuits that can stimulate our minds and foster personal growth. Get ready to dive into the world of lifelong learning, where we'll discover how acquiring new knowledge and skills can boost confidence and open up new horizons. It's time to feed your curiosity and empower your mind!

PART IV

INTELLECTUAL PURSUITS FOR PERSONAL GROWTH

Welcome to Part IV of our journey into empowering pursuits! We've explored creative expression, delved into the world of active hobbies, and discovered the joys of connecting with nature. Now, it's time to turn our attention to the rich and rewarding realm of intellectual pursuits. In this section, we'll explore how engaging your mind in continuous learning and growth can boost your confidence, expand your horizons, and add new dimensions to your life.

THE POWER OF LIFELONG LEARNING

Have you ever felt the thrill of mastering a new skill or the excitement of understanding a complex concept for the first time? That's the magic of intellectual pursuits. They keep our minds sharp, our curiosity alive, and our personal growth ongoing. In a world that's constantly changing, the ability to learn and adapt is not just valuable - it's essential.

Engaging in intellectual hobbies isn't just about acquiring knowledge. It's about challenging yourself, expanding your perspectives, and discovering new passions. Whether you're learning a new language, mastering a musical instrument, or diving into the world of philosophy, you're not just exercising your brain - you're opening doors to new experiences and opportunities.

BOOSTING CONFIDENCE THROUGH KNOWLEDGE

One of the most powerful benefits of intellectual pursuits is the boost they give to your self-confidence. As you acquire new skills and knowledge, you're proving to yourself that you're capable of growth and achievement. This sense of competence often spills over into other areas of life, making you more confident in tackling challenges at work, in relationships, and in your personal goals.

Moreover, intellectual hobbies can provide a sense of purpose and accomplishment that's deeply satisfying. Whether you're solving a complex chess problem, understanding a piece of classical music, or grasping a new scientific concept, there's a unique joy in intellectual achievement.

EXPANDING YOUR WORLDVIEW

Intellectual pursuits have a wonderful way of broadening your perspective on the world. Learning about different cultures through language study, exploring various schools of thought in philosophy, or understanding the intricacies of ecosystems through astronomy - all these can give you a more nuanced and empathetic view of the world around you.

This expanded worldview can make you a more interesting conversationalist, a more effective problem-solver, and a more engaged citizen of the world. It can also lead to a greater sense of connection with others and a deeper appreciation for the diversity of human experience.

THE JOURNEY AHEAD

In the chapters that follow, we'll explore a variety of intellectual pursuits that can enrich your life and empower your mind. From the cognitive benefits of learning a musical instrument to the personal growth that comes from studying a foreign language, we'll discover how these hobbies can transform not just what you know, but who you are.

We'll delve into the strategic thinking of chess and other brain-teasing games, explore the social and intellectual benefits of book clubs, and even gaze at the stars to ponder our place in the universe. Each chapter will provide insights into the benefits of these pursuits, tips for getting started, and inspiration to keep you motivated on your learning journey.

Remember, the goal isn't to become an expert in everything. It's about finding intellectual pursuits that resonate with you, that challenge and excite you, and that help you grow as a person. So open your mind, embrace your curiosity, and get ready to embark on a journey of lifelong learning. Your intellectual adventure starts now!

CHAPTER 21

THE "KNOWLEDGE IS POWER" PRINCIPLE: HOW LEARNING HOBBIES BOOST CONFIDENCE

Have you ever noticed how some people seem to radiate confidence, effortlessly engaging in conversations on a wide range of topics? Chances are, these individuals have embraced the "Knowledge is Power" principle, understanding that continuous learning is a key to personal empowerment. In this chapter, we'll explore how engaging in learning hobbies can dramatically boost your confidence and transform your self-image.

THE CONFIDENCE-KNOWLEDGE CONNECTION

At its core, confidence comes from a sense of competence. When you know you're capable of handling a situation or discussing a topic, you naturally feel more self-assured. This is where learning hobbies come into play. Every new skill you acquire, every piece of knowledge you gain, adds to your toolkit of competence.

Think about the last time you learned something new and were able to apply it. Maybe you picked up a few phrases in a foreign language and successfully ordered a meal on vacation. Or perhaps you learned about a historical event and were able to contribute meaningfully to a discussion. These moments of successfully applying new knowledge give us a confidence boost that can be truly empowering.

BREAKING THE COMFORT ZONE

One of the most powerful aspects of learning hobbies is how they push us out of our comfort zones. When you tackle a new subject or skill, you're venturing into unfamiliar territory. This can be intimidating at first, but it's also where the magic happens. Each time you overcome the initial discomfort and make progress in your learning, you're proving to yourself that you're capable of growth and adaptation.

This willingness to embrace discomfort and challenge yourself can have far-reaching effects. You might find yourself more willing to take on new challenges at work, speak up in social situations, or pursue goals you previously thought were out of reach. The confidence gained from your learning hobbies becomes a transferable skill, empowering you in all areas of life.

THE JOY OF LIFELONG LEARNING

Embracing learning hobbies isn't just about acquiring knowledge for practical purposes. It's about cultivating a love for learning itself. When you approach life with curiosity and a desire to understand more about the world around you, you open yourself up to endless possibilities for growth and enrichment.

This mindset of lifelong learning can be incredibly empowering. It shifts your perspective from "I can't do that" to "I haven't learned how to do that yet." This subtle change in thinking can have a profound impact on your self-confidence and your approach to life's challenges.

FINDING YOUR LEARNING STYLE

As you explore different learning hobbies, you'll likely discover that you have a preferred learning style. Some people are visual learners, thriving on diagrams, charts, and videos. Others are auditory learners, preferring podcasts or lectures. Still others are kinesthetic learners, learning best through hands-on experiences.

Understanding your learning style can boost your confidence by helping you choose hobbies and learning methods that play to your strengths. It can also help you approach new learning challenges more effectively, giving you the tools to tackle even subjects you might have previously found difficult.

THE SOCIAL ASPECT OF LEARNING

Many learning hobbies have a social component that can further boost your confidence. Joining a book club, attending language exchange meetups, or participating in group music lessons all provide opportunities to connect with others who share your interests. These social interactions not only make learning more enjoyable but also allow you to practice sharing your knowledge and skills with others - a great confidence booster in itself.

Moreover, surrounding yourself with fellow learners can be incredibly motivating. You'll be inspired by others' progress and encouraged by the shared experience of growth and discovery. This supportive environment can help you push through challenges and celebrate your achievements, further enhancing your confidence.

EMBRACING THE JOURNEY

As you embark on your learning hobbies, remember that the goal isn't perfection or mastery - it's growth. Every step forward, no matter how small, is a victory worth celebrating. Did you learn one new word in your target language today? Fantastic! Did you finally understand a concept that's been puzzling you? Wonderful! These small wins accumulate over time, building your confidence and reinforcing your identity as a capable, curious learner.

Don't be afraid to make mistakes or ask questions. In fact, view these as essential parts of the learning process. The willingness to admit what you don't know and seek answers is a sign of confidence in itself. It shows that you value growth over the appearance of perfection.

So, are you ready to harness the power of knowledge and boost your confidence? Whether you choose to dive into a new academic subject, learn a practical skill, or explore an artistic pursuit, remember that every moment spent learning is an investment in yourself. You're not just acquiring knowledge - you're building confidence, expanding your horizons, and empowering yourself to tackle whatever life throws your way.

As we continue our exploration of intellectual pursuits, our next chapter will delve into the world of music. Get ready to discover how learning to play a musical instrument can not only provide a creative outlet but also enhance cognitive function and emotional well-being. It's time to tune up your brain and let the music play!

CHAPTER 22

MASTERING A MUSICAL INSTRUMENT: THE COGNITIVE AND EMOTIONAL BENEFITS OF PLAYING MUSIC

Have you ever watched a musician lost in the flow of their performance and felt a twinge of envy? The good news is, you too can experience the joy and benefits of making music. In this chapter, we'll explore how learning to play a musical instrument can boost your brainpower, enhance your emotional well-being, and open up a whole new world of creative expression.

THE BRAIN-BOOSTING POWER OF MUSIC

Learning to play an instrument is like a full-body workout for your brain. It engages multiple areas simultaneously, strengthening neural connections and enhancing cognitive functions. When you play music, you're reading notes, translating them into physical movements, and listening to the output - all at the same time. This complex process can improve your memory, enhance your spatial reasoning, and even boost your mathematical abilities.

Studies have shown that musicians often have better executive function skills, including improved focus, planning, and problem-solving abilities. These skills can translate into other areas of your life, potentially improving your performance at work or in other cognitive tasks. It's no wonder that many successful people in various fields, from science to business, have a background in music!

EMOTIONAL HARMONY: MUSIC AND MENTAL HEALTH

Beyond its cognitive benefits, playing a musical instrument can have a profound impact on your emotional well-being. Music has a unique ability to express and evoke emotions, and as a musician, you gain a powerful tool for emotional release and regulation. Had a stressful day? Sitting down with your instrument can help you process those feelings and find calm.

Learning an instrument also teaches valuable life skills like patience, perseverance, and the ability to handle frustration. As you work through challenging pieces or techniques, you're building resilience that can serve you well in all areas of life. The sense of accomplishment you feel when you finally master a difficult passage can be a significant boost to your self-esteem.

GETTING STARTED: CHOOSING YOUR INSTRUMENT

One of the beautiful things about music is the wide variety of instruments to choose from. Whether you're drawn to the melodic strumming of a guitar, the rhythmic beats of drums, the rich tones of a piano, or the expressive sounds of a violin, there's an instrument out there that will resonate with you.

When selecting an instrument, consider factors like your musical interests, physical capabilities, and practical considerations like space and noise limitations. Don't be afraid to try out different options - many music stores offer rental programs that allow you to experiment before making a commitment.

THE LEARNING JOURNEY: PRACTICE MAKES PROGRESS

Learning a musical instrument is a journey that requires patience and consistent effort. In the beginning, progress might seem slow, and you may feel frustrated at times. This is normal and part of the learning process. Remember, every expert was once a beginner.

Set realistic goals for yourself and celebrate small victories along the way. Maybe your goal this week is to play a simple melody without mistakes, or to practice for 15 minutes each day. These achievable milestones will keep you motivated and help you see your progress over time.

Consider taking lessons, either in-person or online. A good teacher can provide structured learning, correct your technique, and offer encouragement when you need it. They can also introduce you to new musical styles and challenges that will keep your learning journey exciting.

THE SOCIAL SYMPHONY: MAKING MUSIC WITH OTHERS

While solo practice is essential, there's something magical about making music with others. Consider joining a community orchestra, a local band, or even just jamming with friends. Playing music in a group setting not only improves your musical skills but also provides a sense of community and shared accomplishment.

Group music-making can also be a great way to meet new people and build social connections. Whether you're performing in a small ensemble or a large orchestra, you're part of a team working together to create something beautiful. This collaborative aspect of music can be incredibly rewarding and confidence-boosting.

LIFELONG LEARNING: THE NEVER-ENDING MUSICAL JOURNEY

One of the most beautiful aspects of learning a musical instrument is that there's always room for growth. Even professional musicians continue to learn and improve throughout their careers. This means that playing an instrument can be a lifelong source of challenge, growth, and fulfillment.

As you progress, you might find yourself exploring new genres, attempting more complex pieces, or even trying your hand at composition. Each new musical challenge you take on is an opportunity for personal growth and creative expression.

Remember, the goal of learning an instrument isn't to become a world-class performer (unless that's what you want!). It's about enjoying the process of making music, challenging yourself, and reaping the cognitive and emotional benefits along the way. Whether you're strumming a guitar for your own enjoyment or performing Bach for an audience, you're engaging in an activity that nourishes your brain, soothes your soul, and connects you to a rich cultural tradition.

So why not pick up that instrument you've always wanted to try? Your brain will thank you, your heart will sing, and you just might discover a passion that enriches your life in ways you never expected.

As we move from the harmonious world of music, our next chapter will take us on a linguistic adventure. Get ready to explore how learning a new language can open up not just new ways of communication, but new perspectives on the world and yourself. It's time to embark on a journey of words, cultures, and self-discovery!

CHAPTER 23

THE LANGUAGE OF SELF-DISCOVERY: LEARNING A FOREIGN LANGUAGE FOR PERSONAL GROWTH

Have you ever dreamed of ordering coffee in Paris, haggling in a Moroccan bazaar, or chatting with locals in Tokyo? Learning a new language can open up these possibilities and so much more. In this chapter, we'll explore how embarking on a linguistic journey can not only enhance your communication skills but also lead to profound personal growth and self-discovery.

THE COGNITIVE BENEFITS OF BILINGUALISM

Learning a new language is like giving your brain a supercharged workout. It challenges you to think in new ways, grasp unfamiliar concepts, and make connections you've never made before. Studies have shown that bilingual individuals often demonstrate improved cognitive functions, including:

- Enhanced memory and recall
- Better problem-solving skills
- Increased attention span and focus
- Improved decision-making abilities
- Greater mental flexibility and multitasking capabilities

These cognitive benefits can extend far beyond language learning, potentially improving your performance in various aspects of life, from work to personal relationships.

CULTURAL EMPATHY AND GLOBAL UNDERSTANDING

Language and culture are inextricably linked. When you learn a new language, you're not just memorizing vocabulary and grammar rules—you're gaining insight into a different way of thinking and perceiving the world. This exposure to new cultural perspectives can foster empathy, broaden your worldview, and challenge your assumptions about your own culture.

As you progress in your language learning journey, you might find yourself becoming more open-minded and adaptable. You may develop a deeper appreciation for cultural differences and become more adept at navigating diverse social situations. These skills are invaluable in our increasingly globalized world, both personally and professionally.

BOOSTING SELF-CONFIDENCE AND INDEPENDENCE

There's something incredibly empowering about being able to communicate in a foreign language. Each small victory—whether it's successfully ordering a meal or having a brief conversation with a native speaker—can provide a significant boost to your self-confidence. As you become more proficient, you may find yourself more willing to take risks and step out of your comfort zone in other areas of life.

Learning a new language can also foster a sense of independence. Imagine navigating a foreign city, solving problems, and making connections, all in a language that's not your mother tongue. These experiences can help you develop self-reliance and adaptability, valuable traits that translate into all aspects of life.

THE JOURNEY OF SELF-DISCOVERY

Language learning often leads to unexpected self-discoveries. As you grapple with new ways of expressing yourself, you might uncover aspects of your personality that don't come through in your native language. Many language learners report feeling like a slightly different person when speaking their new language—perhaps more outgoing, more reflective, or more humorous.

Moreover, the process of learning a language can teach you a lot about yourself. You'll discover your learning style, test your perseverance, and potentially uncover hidden talents. The challenges and triumphs of language learning can reveal your strengths and areas for growth, contributing to your overall personal development.

GETTING STARTED: CHOOSING YOUR LANGUAGE AND METHOD

Selecting a language to learn is a personal decision. You might be drawn to a language for its cultural significance, professional utility, or simply because you love how it sounds. Consider your goals: Are you learning for travel, work, personal interest, or heritage reasons? Let your motivation guide your choice.

As for learning methods, we're fortunate to live in an age with numerous resources at our fingertips. Traditional classroom settings, language exchange apps, online courses, immersion programs—the options are varied. Experiment with different methods to find what works best for you. Many successful language learners use a combination of approaches to keep their learning engaging and effective.

EMBRACING THE PROCESS

Remember, language learning is a journey, not a destination. It's normal to feel frustrated at times or to hit plateaus in your progress. The key is to stay consistent and find ways to make the process enjoyable. Incorporate your target language into your daily life—watch movies, listen to music, read books, or find a language exchange partner. Celebrate your progress, no matter how small, and don't be afraid to make mistakes. Every error is an opportunity to learn and improve.

As you embark on your language learning adventure, you're not just acquiring a new skill—you're opening doors to new experiences, relationships, and ways of thinking. You're challenging yourself, expanding your horizons, and embarking on a journey of self-discovery that can be truly transformative.

So, whether you're dreaming in French, thinking in Mandarin, or laughing in Spanish, remember that each word you learn is a step towards not just a new language, but a new you. Embrace the journey and watch as your world expands, one word at a time.

As we move from the world of languages, our next chapter will take us into the realm of strategy and cognitive challenge. Get ready to explore the fascinating world of chess and other strategy games. We'll discover how these games can sharpen your mind, improve your decision-making skills, and provide a lifetime of intellectual stimulation. It's time to make your move!

CHAPTER 24

CHESS AND STRATEGY GAMES: SHARPENING YOUR MIND AND DECISION-MAKING SKILLS

Have you ever marveled at the intense concentration of chess players, their minds engaged in an intricate dance of strategy and foresight? Welcome to the world of chess and strategy games, where every move is a decision, every game a lesson, and every player a student of life's most valuable skills. In this chapter, we'll explore how engaging in these mentally stimulating games can sharpen your mind, enhance your decision-making abilities, and provide a lifetime of intellectual growth.

THE MIND-BENDING BENEFITS OF CHESS

Chess, often called the "game of kings," has been challenging and delighting players for centuries. But it's more than just a game—it's a powerful tool for cognitive development. When you sit down at a chessboard, you're not just moving pieces; you're exercising crucial mental muscles.

Playing chess regularly has been shown to improve critical thinking skills, enhance memory and concentration, and boost problem-solving abilities. It teaches you to analyze complex situations, predict outcomes, and plan several steps ahead—skills that are invaluable in many areas of life, from business strategy to personal relationships.

Moreover, chess is a game of patience and perseverance. Learning to stay calm under pressure, to recover from setbacks, and to learn from your mistakes are all part of the chess player's journey. These mental resilience skills can serve you well in facing life's challenges.

BEYOND CHESS: THE WORLD OF STRATEGY GAMES

While chess is perhaps the most well-known strategy game, it's far from the only one. Games like Go, Shogi, and modern board games like Settlers of Catan or Ticket to Ride all offer cognitive benefits. Each game presents its own set of challenges and strategies to master.

For instance, Go, an ancient Chinese game, is known for its vast complexity and emphasis on long-term strategy. It can enhance your ability to see the big picture and think in abstract terms. Modern strategy board games often involve resource management, negotiation, and adapting to changing circumstances—skills that are applicable to many real-world situations.

DECISION-MAKING UNDER PRESSURE

One of the most valuable skills you can gain from strategy games is the ability to make decisions under pressure. In a game of chess or Go, you often have limited time to assess a complex situation and choose the best move. This mirrors many real-life scenarios where we need to make important decisions with incomplete information and time constraints.

As you play more, you'll develop intuition and the ability to quickly evaluate options. You'll learn to balance risk and reward, to think several steps ahead, and to adapt your strategy as circumstances change. These decision-making skills can be invaluable in your personal and professional life.

THE SOCIAL SIDE OF STRATEGY

While many think of chess as a solitary pursuit, strategy games can be social experiences. Joining a chess club, attending game nights, or participating in tournaments can connect you with a diverse community of fellow enthusiasts. These social interactions make the games more enjoyable and provide opportunities to learn from others and share your insights.

Strategy games can also be a great way to build relationships. Whether you're teaching a friend to play, engaging in friendly competition with family, or using games as an icebreaker in professional settings, these shared experiences can strengthen bonds and create lasting memories.

GETTING STARTED: CHOOSING YOUR GAME

If you're new to strategy games, chess is an excellent place to start. Its rules are relatively simple to learn, but its depth ensures you'll always have room to grow and improve. Many online platforms offer free chess lessons and the opportunity to play against opponents of varying skill levels.

However, don't feel limited to chess. Explore different strategy games to find what resonates with you. You might enjoy the territorial aspects of Go, the collaborative elements of some modern board games, or the fast-paced nature of digital strategy games. The key is to find games that challenge and excite you.

THE LEARNING PROCESS: EMBRACING THE CHALLENGE

Learning a strategy game can be intimidating at first. You might feel overwhelmed by the complexity or discouraged by losses. Remember, every expert was once a beginner. Embrace the learning process and focus on improvement rather than winning.

Start with the basics—learn the rules and fundamental strategies. Many games have centuries of theory behind them, but don't let that intimidate you. Focus on understanding fundamental principles rather than memorizing specific moves or strategies. As you play more, you'll naturally start to recognize patterns and develop your own style of play.

Consider studying game analysis or watching expert players. Many online platforms offer the ability to review your games, helping you understand where you can improve. Remember, every game, win or lose, is an opportunity to learn and grow.

INTEGRATING STRATEGY GAMES INTO YOUR LIFE

The beauty of strategy games is that they can fit into almost any lifestyle. A quick online chess game can provide a mental break during a busy workday. A weekend board game session can be a fun social activity. Even just solving chess puzzles for a few minutes a day can help keep your mind sharp.

As you develop your skills, you might find yourself applying game strategies to real-life situations. The ability to think ahead, consider multiple options, and adapt to changing circumstances are all valuable skills in many aspects of life.

Remember, the goal isn't to become a grandmaster (unless that's what you want!). The true value lies in the mental stimulation, the joy of continuous learning, and the applicable life skills you develop along the way. Whether you're checkmating a king, building an empire, or solving complex puzzles, you're also creating a sharper, more strategic mind.

So why not set up a chessboard, download a strategy game app, or invite friends for a board game night? Your brain will thank you for the workout, and you might just discover a lifelong passion for strategic thinking.

As we move from the world of strategy games, our next chapter will take us into shared literary experiences. Get ready to explore the "Book Club Boost" method, where we'll discover how coming together over great books can enhance our understanding, broaden our perspectives, and foster meaningful connections. It's time to turn the page to a new chapter of personal growth through shared reading!

CHAPTER 25

THE "BOOK CLUB BOOST" METHOD: BONDING AND GROWING THROUGH SHARED READING EXPERIENCES

Have you ever finished a great book and felt an overwhelming urge to discuss it with someone? That's the power of literature—it sparks thoughts, emotions, and insights that beg to be shared. Welcome to the world of book clubs, where the joy of reading meets the enrichment of meaningful discussion. In this chapter, we'll explore how joining or starting a book club can enhance your reading experience, broaden your perspectives, and foster deep connections with others.

THE MAGIC OF SHARED READING

Reading is often seen as a solitary activity, but when you join a book club, it transforms into a communal experience. Suddenly, the characters, plots, and themes you've been pondering in private become lively discussion topics. This shared exploration can deepen your understanding of the book and open your eyes to interpretations you might never have considered.

Book clubs offer a unique opportunity to see the world through the eyes of others. As you discuss a book, you'll hear diverse perspectives shaped by different life experiences, cultural backgrounds, and personal beliefs. This exposure to varied viewpoints can broaden your horizons, challenge your assumptions, and foster empathy and understanding.

INTELLECTUAL GROWTH AND CRITICAL THINKING

Participating in book club discussions is like giving your brain a workout. You're honing your critical thinking skills as you articulate your thoughts about the book, defend your interpretations, and consider others' viewpoints. You'll learn to analyze texts more deeply, make connections between ideas, and express your thoughts more clearly.

Moreover, many book clubs read across various genres and subjects, exposing you to books you might not have chosen on your own. This literary diversity can expand your knowledge base, introduce you to new ideas, and perhaps even spark new interests or passions.

THE SOCIAL SIDE OF READING

Book clubs offer more than just intellectual stimulation—they're also a wonderful way to build meaningful social connections. Bonding over shared reading experiences can lead to deep friendships and a sense of community. Whether you're laughing over a humorous passage, debating a character's motivations, or sharing how a book relates to your life, you're creating shared memories and connections.

For many people, book clubs provide a refreshing form of social interaction. Instead of small talk, you dive into substantive discussions about ideas, emotions, and life's big questions. This depth of conversation can be remarkably fulfilling, especially in our often fast-paced, surface-level social world.

GETTING STARTED: JOINING OR CREATING A BOOK CLUB

If you're interested in experiencing the "Book Club Boost," you have two main options: joining an existing club or starting your own. Many libraries, bookstores, and community centers host book clubs that are open to new members. Alternatively, online platforms and social media groups offer virtual book clubs that allow you to connect with readers from around the world.

If you decide to start your own club, begin by inviting friends, colleagues, or neighbors who share your love of reading. Decide on the logistics: how often you'll meet, where (in person or virtually), and how you'll choose books. Some clubs focus on a specific genre, while others read across categories. The key is to create a structure that works for your group.

MAKING THE MOST OF YOUR BOOK CLUB EXPERIENCE

Active participation is key to truly benefit from the "Book Club Boost" method. Here are some tips to enhance your experience:

- **Read actively:** Take notes, underline passages, and jot down questions as you read. This will enrich your own understanding and provide talking points for the discussion.
- **Come prepared:** Finish the book and reflect on it before the meeting. Consider the themes, characters, and any questions you'd like to discuss.
- **Listen actively:** While sharing your thoughts is important, listening to and engaging with others' perspectives is equally valuable.
- **Be open-minded:** You may not always agree with everyone's interpretations, but approaching differences with curiosity rather than judgment can lead to the most insightful discussions.
- **Make connections:** Try to relate the book to your own experiences or current events.

This can lead to more personal and engaging discussions.

BEYOND THE BOOK: EXPANDING YOUR CLUB'S ACTIVITIES

While discussing books is the primary focus, many clubs find ways to enrich their experience further. You might watch film adaptations of the books you read and compare them to the original text. For historical novels, you could plan visits to relevant museums or historical sites. Some clubs even organize themed potlucks based on the book's setting or time period.

These additional activities can add depth to your understanding of the book and provide more opportunities for bonding with your fellow club members.

THE LASTING IMPACT OF BOOK CLUBS

As you engage in the "Book Club Boost" method, you may find that its benefits extend far beyond your reading life. The skills you develop—critical thinking, active listening, articulating your thoughts—can enhance your work performance and personal relationships. The empathy fostered through exploring diverse perspectives can make you more understanding and open-minded in your daily life.

The habit of regular reading and thoughtful discussion can be a powerful antidote to the often superficial nature of modern media consumption. It encourages deeper engagement with ideas and a more reflective approach to the world around you.

So why not embrace the "Book Club Boost" method? Whether discussing a classic novel, a contemporary bestseller, or a thought-provoking non-fiction work, you're not just reading a book—you're embarking on a journey of intellectual growth, social connection, and personal development. Turn the page to this new chapter in your reading life, and watch as it enriches your mind, broadens your perspectives, and deepens your connections with others.

As we close the book on our discussion of literary gatherings, let's set our sights on the vast expanse above us. In our next chapter, we'll explore the awe-inspiring world of astronomy and stargazing.

Get ready to discover how contemplating the cosmos can provide perspective, wonder, and a profound sense of connection to the universe. It's time to look up and explore the stars!

CHAPTER 26

ASTRONOMY AND STARGAZING: FINDING PERSPECTIVE AND WONDER IN THE COSMOS

Have you ever gazed up at a starry night sky and felt a sense of awe? There's something magical about looking into the vastness of space, isn't there? Welcome to the world of astronomy and stargazing, where the universe becomes your playground, and every clear night offers a new adventure. In this chapter, we'll explore how this captivating hobby can provide perspective, inspire wonder, and connect you to the grand cosmic dance we're all part of.

THE UNIVERSAL APPEAL OF STARGAZING

Astronomy is perhaps the oldest of sciences, with humans having looked to the stars for guidance, inspiration, and understanding for millennia. Today, it remains a pursuit that can captivate anyone, regardless of age or background. Whether you're identifying constellations, tracking the phases of the moon, or peering at distant galaxies through a telescope, stargazing offers a unique blend of science, history, and sheer wonder.

One of the most beautiful aspects of astronomy is its accessibility. While advanced equipment can undoubtedly enhance the experience, all you really need to get started is a clear night sky and your own two eyes. This makes it a hobby that's available to almost everyone, anywhere in the world.

GAINING COSMIC PERSPECTIVE

There's nothing quite like contemplating the vastness of the universe to help put our everyday concerns into perspective. When you realize that the light from some stars you're seeing left its source millions of years ago or that each pinprick of light in the night sky could be a sun with its own solar system, it's hard not to feel a sense of awe.

This cosmic perspective can be incredibly grounding. It reminds us that we're part of something much larger than ourselves, our daily worries, and even our planet. Many stargazers report feeling a profound sense of peace and connection to the universe through their observations.

THE SCIENCE OF WONDER

Astronomy offers a unique opportunity to engage with science in a tangible, observable way. As you learn to identify planets, track their movements, and understand phenomena like eclipses or meteor showers, you're not just memorizing facts—you're witnessing the principles of physics and celestial mechanics in action.

This hands-on approach to science can spark curiosity, encourage critical thinking, and foster a deeper appreciation for the scientific method. Whether you're a science enthusiast or someone who's always found it challenging, astronomy provides an engaging entry point into the world of scientific observation and discovery.

GETTING STARTED: YOUR JOURNEY TO THE STARS

Beginning your astronomy journey doesn't require a big investment. Start by familiarizing yourself with the night sky using just your eyes. Learn to identify constellations and bright stars. Apps and star charts can be helpful tools in this process, guiding you through the celestial landscape.

As you progress, you might want to invest in a pair of binoculars or a small telescope. These tools can open up a whole new world, allowing you to see details of the moon's surface, the rings of Saturn, or the moons of Jupiter. Remember, expensive equipment isn't necessary to enjoy astronomy—many seasoned stargazers still enjoy naked-eye observations.

THE SOCIAL SIDE OF STARGAZING

While stargazing can be a peaceful solitary activity, it's also a fantastic way to connect with others. Many communities have astronomy clubs that host star parties—gatherings where enthusiasts set up telescopes and share their knowledge with others. These events can be great opportunities to learn from more experienced stargazers, use different types of equipment, and share in the excitement of celestial discoveries.

Stargazing can also be a beautiful activity to share with family and friends. There's something special about huddling together on a clear night, pointing out constellations, and marveling at the beauty of the cosmos. It's a chance to disconnect from screens and reconnect with each other and the natural world.

ASTRONOMY AND PERSONAL GROWTH

Engaging in astronomy can foster personal growth in unexpected ways. It encourages patience and persistence—after all, sometimes clouds obstruct the view, or it takes practice to locate a particular celestial object. It nurtures a sense of humility, reminding us of our small place in the vast universe. And it can inspire creativity as you contemplate the mysteries of the cosmos and perhaps express your wonder through art, writing, or music.

Astronomy can be a lifelong learning journey. There's always something new to discover, whether it's a deeper understanding of astrophysics, learning astrophotography, or simply observing the changing night sky through the seasons.

As you embark on your stargazing journey, remember that the goal isn't to become an expert astronomer (unless you want to!). It's about cultivating a sense of wonder, gaining perspective, and connecting with the universe in a profound way. Whether you're identifying your first constellation, catching your first glimpse of the Milky Way, or simply enjoying the peace of a starry night, you're participating in a timeless human tradition of looking up and wondering.

So why not step outside tonight and look up? The universe is waiting to share its wonders with you. As you gaze at the stars, remember that you're not just an observer—you're a part of this vast, beautiful cosmos, connected to everything you see in ways we're only beginning to understand.

As we come back down to Earth from our cosmic journey, our next chapter will challenge your mind in a different way. Get ready to dive into the world of puzzles and brain teasers, where we'll discover how these mental gymnastics can keep your mind sharp, boost your problem-solving skills, and provide endless entertainment. It's time to piece together the puzzle of personal development!

CHAPTER 27

THE PUZZLE OF PERSONAL DEVELOPMENT: CROSSWORDS, SUDOKU, AND BRAIN TEASERS

Have you ever felt the rush of satisfaction from solving a challenging puzzle? That moment when the last crossword clue clicks into place or when you pencil in the final number in a Sudoku grid? Welcome to the world of puzzles and brain teasers, where every solved challenge is a small victory for your cognitive skills. In this chapter, we'll explore how engaging with these mental gymnastics can sharpen your mind, enhance your problem-solving abilities, and provide a fun path to personal growth.

THE COGNITIVE BENEFITS OF PUZZLE-SOLVING

Puzzles are more than just a fun way to pass the time—they're a workout for your brain. Engaging regularly with puzzles like crosswords, Sudoku, or logic problems can have significant cognitive benefits. These activities challenge different parts of your brain, promoting mental flexibility and helping to keep your mind sharp as you age.

Crossword puzzles, for instance, exercise your language skills and semantic memory. They require you to recall a broad range of knowledge and make connections between seemingly unrelated concepts. Sudoku, on the other hand, hones your logical thinking and pattern recognition skills. It trains you to look at a problem from multiple angles and use deductive reasoning to find solutions.

PROBLEM-SOLVING BEYOND THE PUZZLE

The skills you develop through puzzle-solving don't just stay on the page—they can translate into real-life problem-solving abilities. As you tackle increasingly complex puzzles, you're training your brain to approach challenges methodically, break problems into manageable parts, and persist in the face of difficulty.

These skills can be invaluable in your personal and professional life. Whether you're troubleshooting a work issue, managing a household budget, or navigating a personal dilemma, the analytical thinking and patience you've honed through puzzles can come into play.

STRESS RELIEF AND MINDFULNESS

In our fast-paced, constantly connected world, puzzles offer a unique form of stress relief. When you're focused on solving a crossword or completing a jigsaw puzzle, you enter a state of flow that can be deeply relaxing. This focused attention acts as a form of meditation, allowing you to temporarily set aside your worries and immerse yourself in the present moment.

Moreover, the sense of accomplishment you get from solving a puzzle can boost your mood and self-confidence. Each solved puzzle is a small victory, a reminder of your capabilities that can help counteract stress and negative self-talk.

GETTING STARTED: CHOOSING YOUR PUZZLE

The world of puzzles is vast and varied, offering something for every interest and skill level. Here are a few popular options to consider:

- **Crosswords:** Great for language-lovers and trivia buffs.
- **Sudoku:** Perfect for those who enjoy logic and numbers.
- **Jigsaw puzzles:** Ideal for visual thinkers and those who enjoy tactile challenges.

- **Logic puzzles:** Excellent for developing deductive reasoning skills.
- **Word searches:** A more relaxed option that still exercises your attention to detail.

Start with puzzles at a comfortable difficulty level and gradually challenge yourself with harder ones as your skills improve. Remember, the goal is to challenge yourself while still having fun.

MAKING PUZZLES A DAILY HABIT

Incorporating puzzles into your daily routine can be a great way to ensure consistent mental exercise. You might start your day with a crossword over breakfast, unwind in the evening with a Sudoku, or keep a book of brain teasers handy for your commute or lunch break.

Many newspapers and websites offer daily puzzles, making it easy to incorporate this habit into your routine. There are also numerous puzzle apps available, allowing you to engage in mental exercise wherever you go.

THE SOCIAL SIDE OF PUZZLING

While often seen as a solitary activity, puzzles can also be a great way to connect with others. Solving crosswords or tackling a large jigsaw puzzle with friends or family can be a fun, low-pressure way to spend time together. Many communities have puzzle clubs or meetups where enthusiasts gather to solve puzzles collaboratively.

Online communities also offer opportunities to connect with fellow puzzle lovers. You can share tips, discuss challenging clues, or participate in puzzle-solving competitions.

PUZZLES AND LIFELONG LEARNING

One of the beautiful aspects of puzzling is that it encourages lifelong learning. Crosswords, for instance, often introduce you to new words, historical facts, or cultural references. As you solve more puzzles, you're constantly expanding your knowledge base.

This aspect of puzzling can be particularly beneficial as we age. Engaging in mentally stimulating activities like puzzle-solving has been linked to better cognitive function in older adults. It may even help reduce the risk of cognitive decline.

As you embark on your puzzling journey, remember that the true value lies not just in solving the puzzle but in enjoying the process. Don't get discouraged if you can't immediately solve a challenging puzzle—each attempt is exercising your brain and building your skills.

Whether you're decoding a cryptic crossword clue, fitting together puzzle pieces, or cracking a brain teaser, you're doing more than just passing the time. You're engaging in mental exercise that can enhance your cognitive abilities, reduce stress, and provide a sense of accomplishment.

So why not pick up a puzzle book, download a puzzle app, or challenge a friend to a crossword competition? Your brain will thank you for the workout, and you might just discover a new passion that keeps your mind sharp and your days more engaging.

As we solve the final clue in our exploration of puzzles, let's turn our attention to the social side of hobbies. In our next chapter, we'll discover how shared interests can lead to meaningful connections and a sense of community. Get ready to explore the "Social Hobby Butterfly" effect and learn how your passions can become bridges to new friendships and experiences. It's time to connect the dots between personal interests and social bonds!

PART V

SOCIAL HOBBIES FOR CONNECTION AND COMMUNITY

Welcome to Part V of our journey into empowering pursuits! We've explored creative expression, delved into active hobbies, discovered the joys of intellectual pursuits. Now it's time to turn our attention to the social side of personal growth. In this section, we'll explore how hobbies can become powerful tools for building connections, fostering community, and enriching our social lives.

THE POWER OF SHARED INTERESTS

Humans are inherently social creatures, and there's something magical about connecting with others over shared passions. Whether you're discussing a book in a reading group, collaborating on a community service project, or cheering on your team in a sports league, shared activities create a unique bond. These connections can lead to lasting friendships, professional networks, and a sense of belonging that enriches our lives in countless ways.

BREAKING OUT OF SOCIAL COMFORT ZONES

For many of us, especially in adulthood, making new friends and expanding our social circles can feel challenging. Social hobbies provide a natural, low-pressure way to meet like-minded people. When you're engaged in an activity you enjoy, conversations flow more easily, and common ground is already established. This can be particularly valuable for introverts or those who find traditional socializing overwhelming.

BUILDING COMMUNITY IN A DIGITAL AGE

In our increasingly digital world, social hobbies offer a refreshing opportunity for face-to-face interactions and real-world community building. While online connections have their place, there's something irreplaceable about sharing experiences in person, whether cooking together, playing team sports, or crafting side by side.

THE JOURNEY AHEAD

In the following chapters, we'll explore a variety of social hobbies that can help you expand your social network, deepen existing relationships, and find your tribe. From the camaraderie of team sports to the shared purpose of volunteering, from the lively discussions of book clubs to the creative collaborations in craft circles, we'll discover how these activities can become gateways to richer, more connected lives.

Remember, the goal isn't to become a social butterfly overnight or to fill every moment with group activities. It's about finding meaningful ways to connect with others that align with your interests and values. Whether you're an extrovert energized by constant interaction or an introvert who prefers smaller, more intimate gatherings, there's a social hobby out there for you.

So get ready to step out, reach out, and connect. Your next great friendship, future community, or new support network might be just a shared hobby away. Let's embark on this journey of social discovery together!

CHAPTER 28

THE "SOCIAL HOBBY BUTTERFLY" EFFECT: HOW HOBBIES HELP YOU MAKE FRIENDS

Have you ever noticed how some people seem to effortlessly attract friends and build connections wherever they go? Often, these social butterflies have a secret weapon: their hobbies. Welcome to the world of the "Social Hobby Butterfly," where shared interests become the wings that carry you into new friendships and vibrant communities. In this chapter, we'll explore how pursuing hobbies can transform your social life, helping you forge meaningful connections and expand your circle of friends.

THE MAGIC OF SHARED INTERESTS

There's something almost magical about bonding over a shared passion. When you engage in a hobby with others, you're not just participating in an activity—you're creating a common ground that can serve as the foundation for friendship. Whether you're discussing the latest bestseller in a book club, collaborating on a community garden project, or cheering for your team in a recreational sports league, these shared experiences create an instant connection.

This shared interest provides a natural conversation starter, breaking down the awkwardness of meeting new people. You already have something in common, something to talk about, and a reason to continue interacting. It's like having a built-in ice-breaker wherever you go.

BREAKING OUT OF SOCIAL COMFORT ZONES

For many of us, especially as adults, making new friends can feel daunting. We might worry about what to say, how to approach people, or whether we'll fit in. This is where the "Social Hobby Butterfly" effect really shines. When you're engaged in a hobby you love, you're likely to be more relaxed, more authentic, and more open to new connections.

Moreover, hobbies provide a structured environment for socializing. Instead of the pressure of making small talk at a party, you're focused on the activity at hand. This shared focus can make interactions feel more natural and less forced. Before you know it, you might find yourself chatting easily with people you've just met, bonding over your shared interests.

FINDING YOUR TRIBE

One of the most powerful aspects of the "Social Hobby Butterfly" effect is its ability to help you find your tribe—people who share your passions, values, and interests. In a world where it's easy to feel isolated or misunderstood, connecting with like-minded individuals can be affirming and energizing.

These connections often extend beyond the hobby itself. The friends you make through shared interests might become part of your broader support network, offering companionship, advice, and emotional support in various aspects of life. Many people find that some of their closest, most enduring friendships started through a shared hobby.

EXPANDING YOUR SOCIAL HORIZONS

Engaging in social hobbies doesn't just help you make friends—it can also broaden your social horizons. You might find yourself interacting with people from different age groups, cultural backgrounds, or walks of life that you wouldn't normally encounter in your day-today routine. This diversity can enrich your life, exposing you to new perspectives and experiences.

As you become more involved in your hobby communities, you might discover opportunities for leadership or mentorship. Organizing events, teaching newcomers, or taking on responsibilities within a club can further enhance your social skills and expand your network.

THE RIPPLE EFFECT OF SOCIAL CONNECTIONS

The "Social Hobby Butterfly" effect often creates a positive ripple in your life. As you make friends through one hobby, you might be introduced to new interests and activities through these connections. Your social network grows, your experiences diversify, and your life becomes richer and more fulfilling.

Additionally, having a robust social network has been linked to numerous health benefits, including reduced stress, improved mental health, and increased longevity. By fostering connections through your hobbies, you're not just enriching your social life—you're improving your overall well-being.

EMBRACING YOUR INNER SOCIAL HOBBY BUTTERFLY

Remember, becoming a "Social Hobby Butterfly" doesn't mean you need to transform into an extrovert overnight. It's about finding the right balance that works for you. Start small if you're feeling hesitant. Attend a local meetup related to your hobby, join an online community, or invite a colleague who shares your interest to engage in the hobby together.

The key is approaching your hobbies with an open mind and a willingness to connect. Be genuine in your interactions, show interest in others, and don't be afraid to share your own experiences and knowledge. Over time, you'll likely find that your social circles naturally expand as you flutter from one shared interest to another.

So, are you ready to spread your social wings? Whether you're joining a hiking club, attending a knitting circle, or participating in a community theater production, remember that each shared experience is an opportunity for connection. Embrace your passions, be open to new friendships, and watch as the "Social Hobby Butterfly" effect transforms your social life, one shared interest at a time.

As we flutter away from the world of social hobbies, our next chapter will guide us toward making a positive impact in our communities. Get ready to explore the rewarding world of volunteering and community service. We'll discover how giving back can not only benefit others but also provide a profound sense of purpose and connection in your own life. It's time to spread your wings and make a difference!

CHAPTER 29

VOLUNTEERING AND COMMUNITY SERVICE: FINDING FULFILLMENT THROUGH GIVING BACK

Have you ever experienced the warm glow of satisfaction that comes from helping others? That feeling of making a real difference in someone's life or in your community? Welcome to the world of volunteering and community service, where your time and efforts can create ripples of positive change. In this chapter, we'll explore how giving back can not only benefit others but also provide you with a profound sense of purpose, connection, and personal growth.

THE POWER OF GIVING BACK

Volunteering is more than just free labor—it's a powerful force for good that benefits both the giver and the receiver. When you volunteer, you're both helping to address societal needs and also investing in your own well-being. Studies have shown that regular volunteering can lead to improved mental health, increased life satisfaction, and even better physical health.

However, perhaps the most significant benefit of volunteering is the sense of purpose it can provide. In our often self-focused world, reaching out to help others can give you a broader perspective and a feeling of being part of something larger than yourself. It's a reminder that we're all interconnected and that our actions can have a meaningful impact on the world around us.

FINDING YOUR VOLUNTEERING NICHE

One of the beautiful things about volunteering is the sheer variety of opportunities available. Whether you're passionate about environmental conservation, animal welfare, education, healthcare, or social justice, there's likely a volunteering opportunity that aligns with your interests and values. Here are just a few possibilities to consider:

- Environmental cleanup and conservation projects
- Tutoring or mentoring programs for youth
- Animal shelter support
- Food banks and soup kitchens
- Elderly care and companionship programs
- Disaster relief efforts
- Cultural institutions like museums or libraries

The key is to find a cause that resonates with you personally. When you're passionate about your work, volunteering doesn't feel like a chore—it becomes a fulfilling part of your life.

BUILDING SKILLS AND EXPANDING HORIZONS

Volunteering isn't just about what you give—it's also about what you gain. Many volunteer roles offer opportunities to learn new skills, gain valuable experience, and even explore potential career paths. Whether you're developing leadership skills by organizing events, honing your communication abilities through public speaking, or learning practical skills like grant writing or project management, volunteering can be a fantastic way to grow personally and professionally.

Moreover, volunteering often exposes you to diverse groups of people and new perspectives. This exposure can broaden your worldview, increase your empathy, and help you develop a deeper understanding of social issues and community needs.

THE SOCIAL SIDE OF SERVICE

Community service is inherently social, providing ample opportunities to connect with like-minded individuals who share your values and passion for making a difference. These connections can lead to lasting friendships, professional networking opportunities, and a sense of belonging to a community of changemakers.

Many volunteers find that the relationships they build through service become an essential part of their social support network. There's something special about bonding with others over shared efforts to improve your community or help those in need.

OVERCOMING BARRIERS TO VOLUNTEERING

Despite the many benefits of volunteering, it's common to face barriers that might hold you back. Time constraints, uncertainty about where to start, or feelings of inadequacy are all normal concerns. Remember, even small contributions can make a big difference. Start with short-term or one-time volunteer opportunities if you're unsure about making a long-term commitment.

Many organizations offer flexible volunteering options, including virtual opportunities that you can do from home. Don't be afraid to reach out to organizations you're interested in—they're often happy to work with volunteers to find roles that fit their skills and availability.

MAKING VOLUNTEERING A SUSTAINABLE PART OF YOUR LIFE

To truly reap the benefits of volunteering, it's important to approach it as a long-term part of your life rather than a one-off activity. Here are some tips for making volunteering a sustainable practice:

- Start small and gradually increase your commitment as you find your niche.
- Set realistic goals for your volunteering efforts to avoid burnout.
- Reflect on your experiences and the impact you're making to stay motivated.
- Be open to trying different types of volunteering until you find what feels most fulfilling.
- Involve friends or family to make it a shared experience and keep each other accountable.

Remember, the goal isn't to save the world single-handedly but to contribute positively in ways that are meaningful to you and sustainable for your lifestyle.

As you embark on your volunteering journey, keep in mind that every act of service, no matter how small, has the potential to create positive change. Your efforts ripple outward, touching lives in ways you might never fully see or understand. By giving your time and energy to causes you care about, you're not just helping others—you're enriching your own life, expanding your horizons, and becoming part of a larger community of individuals working towards a better world.

So, are you ready to roll up your sleeves and make a difference? Whether you're serving meals at a local shelter, planting trees in your community, or offering your professional skills to a non-profit organization, remember that your contribution matters. Embrace the opportunity to give back, and watch as it transforms not just your community but your sense of purpose and connection to the world around you.

As we move from individual acts of service to group activities, our next chapter will explore the vibrant world of team sports and fitness groups. Get ready to discover how joining forces with others in physical pursuits can boost your health, expand your social circle, and ignite a spirit of camaraderie. It's time to lace up those sneakers and experience the power of team spirit!

CHAPTER 30

THE "TEAM SPIRIT" TACTIC: JOINING SPORTS LEAGUES AND FITNESS GROUPS

Have you ever felt the rush of excitement when your team scores a goal or the sense of camaraderie as you push through a challenging workout with a group of friends? Welcome to team sports and fitness groups, where physical activity meets social connection. In this chapter, we'll explore how joining sports leagues and fitness groups can not only improve your health but also expand your social circle and boost your overall well-being.

THE POWER OF TEAM SPIRIT

There's something uniquely invigorating about being part of a team or fitness community. Whether you're playing in a recreational soccer league, joining a running club, or participating in group fitness classes, the energy of collective effort can push you to new heights. This "team spirit" isn't just about achieving fitness goals. It's also a way to build connections, foster support, and create a sense of belonging.

When you're part of a team or fitness group, you're not just working on your physical health. You're also developing social skills, learning to communicate effectively, and building trust with others. These experiences can translate into improved relationships and social confidence in other areas of your life.

FINDING YOUR FITNESS TRIBE

One of the beautiful things about sports and fitness is the sheer variety of options available. From traditional team sports like basketball or volleyball to more niche activities like ultimate frisbee or rock climbing, there's likely a sport or fitness activity out there that aligns with your interests and abilities. Here are a few popular options to consider:

- Recreational sports leagues (soccer, basketball, softball, etc.)
- Running or cycling clubs
- Group fitness classes (yoga, Zumba, CrossFit, etc.)
- Outdoor adventure groups (hiking, kayaking, rock climbing)
- Dance classes or teams

The key is to find an activity that you enjoy, and that fits your schedule and fitness level. Remember, the goal is not just physical fitness but also social connection and enjoyment.

BREAKING DOWN BARRIERS

For many people, the idea of joining a sports team or fitness group can be intimidating, especially if you're new to the activity or feel out of shape. It's important to remember that many recreational leagues and fitness groups welcome participants of all skill levels. In fact, these groups often provide a supportive environment for beginners to learn and improve.

If you're feeling hesitant, start by observing a game or class before joining. Many groups offer "try it out" sessions for newcomers. Remember, everyone was a beginner at some point, and most people in these groups are there for fun and fitness, not intense competition.

THE SOCIAL BENEFITS OF SWEATING TOGETHER

One of the most powerful aspects of team sports and group fitness is the social connections they foster. When you're working toward common goals, supporting each other through challenges, and celebrating victories together, you're building bonds that can extend beyond the field or gym.

Many people find that their sports teams or fitness groups become an important part of their social circle. Post-game gatherings, weekend hikes, or just chatting before and after classes can lead to meaningful friendships. These shared experiences and mutual support create a unique kind of camaraderie that's hard to replicate in other settings.

BOOSTING MENTAL HEALTH THROUGH GROUP ACTIVITY

While the physical health benefits of sports and fitness are well-known, the mental health benefits of group activities are equally important. Regular exercise is known to reduce stress, anxiety, and depression, and these effects can be amplified when you're exercising with others.

The social support, sense of belonging, and regular interaction that come with being part of a team or fitness group can significantly improve your mood and overall mental well-being. Many people find that their sports or fitness communities become a crucial part of their support network, providing encouragement and positivity both on and off the field.

BALANCING COMPETITION AND FUN

While some people thrive on competition, others prefer a more relaxed approach to sports and fitness. The beauty of recreational leagues and fitness groups is that they often cater to a range of preferences. Whether you're looking for friendly competition or just a fun way to stay active, there's likely a group that fits your style.

Remember, the primary goal of these activities is enjoyment and personal growth. Focus on your own progress and the joy of the activity rather than comparing yourself to others or obsessing over winning.

As you embark on your journey into team sports or group fitness, keep an open mind and be patient with yourself. Finding the right activity or group that fits your personality and goals might take some time. Don't be afraid to try different things until you find what resonates with you.

Remember, joining a sports league or fitness group is about more than just physical exercise. It's about challenging yourself, making new connections, and becoming part of a community. Whether you're scoring goals on the soccer field, mastering a new yoga pose, or completing a group hike, you're not just improving your health—you're enriching your life with new experiences and friendships.

So, are you ready to embrace the "team spirit" and discover the joy of sweating together? Lace up those sneakers, grab that water bottle, and step into the vibrant world of group sports and fitness. Your body, mind, and social life will thank you for it!

As we move from the energetic world of sports and fitness, let's turn our attention to another form of creative community. In our next chapter, we'll explore the world of crafting circles, where hands-on creativity meets social connection. Get ready to discover how shared crafting experiences can nurture both your artistic side and your social bonds. It's time to weave together the threads of creativity and companionship!

CHAPTER 31

THE SISTERHOOD OF CRAFTING: KNITTING CIRCLES, QUILTING BEES, AND MORE

Have you ever felt the satisfaction of creating something beautiful with your own hands, surrounded by a circle of friends doing the same? Welcome to the world of crafting circles, where creativity and community intertwine like threads in a tapestry. In this chapter, we'll explore how joining or forming a crafting group can not only nurture your artistic side but also weave strong bonds of friendship and support.

THE MAGIC OF CREATING TOGETHER

There's something uniquely powerful about crafting in a group. Whether knitting, quilting, scrapbooking, or engaging in any other hands-on, creative pursuit, doing it alongside others adds a special dimension to the experience. The shared focus on creation fosters a relaxed, supportive atmosphere where conversation flows easily, and friendships naturally develop.

Crafting circles have a rich history, from traditional quilting bees to modern-day stitch 'n bitch groups. These gatherings have long served as spaces for women (and increasingly, people of all genders) to come together, share skills, and support one another while creating beautiful and useful items.

FINDING YOUR CRAFTY TRIBE

One of the beautiful things about crafting circles is the variety of options available. Here are just a few types of groups you might explore:

- Knitting or crochet circles
- Quilting bees
- Scrapbooking groups
- Embroidery or cross-stitch clubs
- Painting or drawing groups
- Jewelry-making circles

Don't worry if you're a beginner—many crafting groups welcome members of all skill levels. In fact, these groups can be excellent places to learn new skills, with more experienced members often happy to share their knowledge and tips.

THE BENEFITS BEYOND THE CRAFT

While the primary focus of these groups is on the craft itself, the benefits extend far beyond the finished products. Crafting circles provide a unique form of social support, offering a regular opportunity to connect with others in a low-pressure environment. The rhythmic, meditative nature of many crafts can also have a calming effect, making these gatherings a great way to de-stress and unwind.

Moreover, crafting circles often become a source of emotional support and friendship. As hands are busy with needles, hooks, or brushes, conversations naturally flow, covering everything from daily life challenges to deeper personal issues. Many women find that their crafting group becomes a vital part of their support network.

STARTING YOUR OWN CRAFTING CIRCLE

If you can't find an existing group that fits your interests or schedule, why not start your own? Begin by reaching out to friends, family, or colleagues who share your crafting interests. You could also post notices in local craft stores, community centers, or online forums to attract like-minded individuals.

When organizing your group, consider factors like meeting frequency, location (homes, cafes, community spaces), and whether you want to focus on a specific project or allow members to work on individual pieces. Remember, the key is to create a welcoming, relaxed atmosphere where creativity and conversation can flourish.

THE JOY OF SKILL SHARING

One of the most rewarding aspects of crafting circles is the opportunity to learn from others and share your skills. You might pick up a new technique for turning a heel in knitting, learn a clever way to organize your scrapbooking materials or discover a whole new craft you'd never considered trying before.

This exchange of knowledge not only enhances your crafting skills and fosters a sense of community and mutual support. There's a special kind of bond that forms when you teach someone a skill or learn something new from a fellow crafter.

CRAFTING FOR A CAUSE

Many crafting circles find additional meaning and purpose by creating items for charitable causes. Whether it's knitting hats for premature babies, making quilts for homeless shelters, or crafting items to sell for fundraisers, these projects can add a sense of greater purpose to your crafting gatherings.

Crafting for others can be incredibly fulfilling, knowing that your creations will bring comfort or joy to those in need. It's a beautiful way to extend the warmth and care of your crafting circle out into the wider community.

As you embark on your journey into the world of crafting circles, remember that the true value lies not just in the items you create but in the connections you form and the joy you share. Whether you're a seasoned crafter or a curious beginner, this warm and welcoming community has a place for you.

So, why not pick up those knitting needles, thread that quilting needle, or grab your scrapbooking supplies? Whether you're joining an established group or starting your own crafting circle, you're not just creating beautiful objects—you're weaving a tapestry of friendship, support, and shared creativity that can enrich your life in countless ways.

As we tie off the last stitch in our exploration of crafting circles, let's turn our attention to another form of creative gathering. In our next chapter, we'll delve into cooking classes and supper clubs, where the joy of creating extends to the culinary arts. Get ready to discover how shared meals can become a recipe for friendship and cultural exploration. It's time to don your apron and savor the flavors of community!

CHAPTER 32

COOKING CLASSES AND SUPPER CLUBS: CONNECTING THROUGH CULINARY ADVENTURES

Have you ever noticed how food has a magical way of bringing people together? Whether gathering around a family dinner table or exploring new flavors with friends, sharing a meal creates connections like nothing else. In this chapter, we'll dive into the delicious world of cooking classes and supper clubs, exploring how these culinary adventures can spice up your social life, broaden your cultural horizons, and satisfy your appetite for both good food and meaningful connections.

THE RECIPE FOR SOCIAL CONNECTION

Cooking classes and supper clubs offer a unique blend of learning, creativity, and social interaction. Unlike traditional restaurants, where the focus is solely on eating, these gatherings put the process of creating and sharing food at the center of the experience. This shared activity provides a natural icebreaker and a common ground for conversation, making it easier to connect with others, even if you're naturally shy or introverted.

COOKING CLASSES: STIRRING UP NEW SKILLS AND FRIENDSHIPS

Imagine standing side by side with a group of fellow food enthusiasts, all eager to learn how to roll the perfect sushi or master the art of

French pastry. Cooking classes offer more than just culinary skills. They also provide a shared experience that can be the foundation for new friendships.

These classes come in all flavors, from one-off workshops on specific cuisines to ongoing series that delve deep into cooking techniques. Many local culinary schools, community centers, and even high-end restaurants offer classes for home cooks. The key is to find a class that aligns with your interests and skill level.

SUPPER CLUBS: DINING WITH A TWIST

Supper clubs take the concept of dining out and add a dash of adventure and a pinch of exclusivity. These gatherings can range from underground restaurants hosted in someone's home to organized events in unique locations. The common thread is the emphasis on shared experiences and, often, the opportunity to try cuisines or dishes that aren't readily available in traditional restaurants.

Joining a supper club can be an excellent way to expand your social circle while indulging your foodie passions. You'll often find yourself seated with strangers who quickly become friends as you bond over the shared culinary journey.

CULTURAL EXPLORATION THROUGH CUISINE

One of the beautiful aspects of cooking classes and supper clubs is their ability to act as a gateway to different cultures. Through food, you can travel the world without leaving your city. Whether you're learning to make authentic Thai curry, participating in a traditional Japanese tea ceremony, or enjoying a feast of Middle Eastern mezze, these experiences offer insights into diverse cultures and traditions.

This cultural exploration through food can broaden your perspectives, foster empathy, and even inspire future travel plans. It's a delicious way to become a more globally-minded citizen.

OVERCOMING KITCHEN JITTERS

If the idea of cooking in front of others makes you nervous, remember that many people in cooking classes feel the same way. The focus is on learning and enjoying the process, not being a master chef. Most instructors are adept at creating a supportive, non-judgmental environment where it's okay to make mistakes and ask questions.

For those who prefer a more passive role, many supper clubs offer events where you can enjoy expertly prepared meals without having to cook yourself. These can be a great way to dip your toe into the culinary social scene before diving into participatory events.

STARTING YOUR OWN CULINARY COMMUNITY

Feeling inspired to create your own culinary gathering? Consider starting a rotating dinner party group with friends, where each person takes turns hosting and preparing a meal. Or organize a themed potluck series, where everyone brings a dish related to a specific cuisine or ingredient.

If you're more ambitious, you might even consider hosting your own supper club events. This can be a fantastic way to share your passion for cooking while creating a unique social experience for others.

NURTURING RELATIONSHIPS OVER SHARED MEALS

There's something intimate and bonding about preparing and sharing food together. The conversations that happen while chopping vegetables or waiting for a dish to come out of the oven often lead to deeper connections than those in more formal social settings.

Many people find that the friendships formed in cooking classes or supper clubs extend beyond the kitchen. You might discover a new best friend, a potential business partner, or even a romantic connection, all sparked by a shared love of food.

As you embark on your culinary social adventures, remember that the joy is in the journey as much as the destination (or, in this case, the meal). Whether you're mastering a new cooking technique, discovering a favorite dish from another culture, or simply enjoying good company over a shared meal, you're nourishing not just your body but your social connections and cultural understanding as well.

So, why not spice up your social life with some culinary exploration? Whether you're wielding a whisk in a cooking class or savoring unique dishes at a supper club, you're not just eating—you're creating memories, forging friendships, and expanding your world, one delicious bite at a time.

As we clear the table from our culinary adventures, let's prepare for a journey of a different kind. In our next chapter, we'll explore how travel can become a social activity, bringing people together through shared experiences and discoveries. Get ready to pack your bags and join the "Travel Tribe" as we discover how group trips can lead to lifelong friendships and unforgettable adventures!

CHAPTER 33

THE "TRAVEL TRIBE" TECHNIQUE: BONDING WITH FELLOW ADVENTURERS ON GROUP TRIPS

Have you ever dreamed of exploring ancient ruins, trekking through lush jungles, or immersing yourself in vibrant foreign cultures, all while forging deep connections with like-minded adventurers? Welcome to the world of group travel, where shared experiences and discoveries create bonds that can last a lifetime. In this chapter, we'll explore how joining or organizing group trips can expand your social circle, push your boundaries, and create memories that will have you reminiscing for years to come.

THE MAGIC OF SHARED ADVENTURES

There's something uniquely powerful about experiencing new places and cultures alongside others. When you travel with a group, every awe-inspiring vista, every challenging hike, every delicious local delicacy becomes a shared memory. These collective experiences create a special kind of bond, often leading to friendships that transcend the usual barriers of age, background, or nationality.

Group travel also offers a built-in support system. Navigating unfamiliar territories or overcoming travel hiccups becomes easier when you have a team to lean on. This shared problem-solving and mutual support can quickly turn strangers into trusted companions.

FINDING YOUR TRAVEL TRIBE

The beauty of group travel is that there's something for every interest and comfort level. Whether you're drawn to active adventures, cultural immersions, foodie tours, or wellness retreats, there's likely a group trip that aligns with your passions. Here are a few types of group travel experiences to consider:

- Adventure tours (hiking, cycling, kayaking)
- Cultural exploration trips
- Volunteer vacations
- Culinary tours
- Photography expeditions
- Wellness and yoga retreats

When choosing a group trip, consider factors like group size, activity level, and the balance between structured activities and free time. Some travelers prefer the intimacy of small group tours, while others enjoy the energy of larger groups.

BREAKING OUT OF YOUR COMFORT ZONE

One of the greatest benefits of group travel is how it gently pushes you out of your comfort zone. Surrounded by the support of your fellow travelers, you might find yourself trying activities you'd never attempt alone—whether it's sampling exotic street food, attempting a challenging hike, or striking up a conversation with locals in a new language.

These shared challenges and triumphs create lasting memories and foster personal growth. Many travelers return home with increased confidence, adaptability, and openness to new experiences.

CULTURAL UNDERSTANDING THROUGH SHARED DISCOVERY

Group travel offers a unique opportunity to deepen your understanding of different cultures. As you and your travel companions navigate new customs, try local cuisines, and interact with people from diverse backgrounds, you're not just observing—you're actively engaging with the world around you.

The discussions and reflections that naturally arise within your travel group can enhance this cultural learning. Different perspectives from your fellow travelers can provide new insights and challenge your assumptions, leading to a more nuanced understanding of the places you visit.

OVERCOMING TRAVEL ANXIETY

For those who feel anxious about traveling alone, group trips can provide a perfect middle ground between solo travel and vacationing with friends or family. The structure and support of a group can alleviate common travel worries, from logistical concerns to safety issues.

Moreover, traveling with a group of like-minded individuals can be less intimidating than striking out on your own, especially in destinations that feel very different from home. It's a way to step out of your comfort zone while still having a safety net.

EXTENDING CONNECTIONS BEYOND THE TRIP

One of the most rewarding aspects of group travel is how the connections formed can extend far beyond the duration of the trip. Many travelers find that they stay in touch with their "travel tribe" long after returning home. These friendships can lead to future travel plans together, reunions, or simply a global network of friends to visit or connect with.

In our increasingly digital world, it's easier than ever to maintain these connections. Social media groups, shared photo albums, and video calls can help keep the travel bonds alive, allowing you to relive memories and plan new adventures together.

153

CREATING YOUR OWN TRAVEL TRIBE

Inspired to organize your own group trip? Start by reaching out to friends, family, or colleagues who share your travel interests. Consider choosing a destination or theme that resonates with your group, and don't be afraid to invite friends of friends to expand your circle.

When planning, aim for a balance between structured activities and free time. Some of the best moments in group travel often happen during unplanned explorations or leisurely meals together.

As you embark on your group travel adventures, remember that the true value lies not just in the destinations you visit but in the connections you form and the personal growth you experience. Whether you're marveling at the wonders of the world, navigating the streets of a bustling foreign city, or sharing quiet moments of reflection with your new friends, you're not just traveling—you're expanding your world and your circle of connections in profound ways.

So, are you ready to join the "Travel Tribe"? Pack your bags, open your heart to new experiences and friendships, and get ready to explore the world alongside fellow adventurers. The journey of a thousand miles begins with a single step—and it's even better when you take that step with new friends by your side.

As we return from our globetrotting adventures, let's shift our focus to finding peace and relaxation closer to home. In our next chapter, we'll explore how creating a dedicated space for your hobbies can enhance your enjoyment and deepen your practice. Get ready to discover the "Hobby Haven" method, where we'll learn how to carve out a personal oasis for creativity and relaxation in your home. It's time to create a space that nurtures your passions and refreshes your spirit!

PART VI

HOBBIES FOR STRESS RELIEF AND RELAXATION

Welcome to Part VI of our journey into empowering pursuits! We've explored creative expression, active hobbies, intellectual pursuits, and social connections. Now, it's time to focus on perhaps one of the most vital aspects of personal well-being: stress relief and relaxation. In this section, we'll discover how hobbies can become powerful tools for managing stress, finding inner calm, and nurturing a sense of peace in our often hectic lives.

THE POWER OF MINDFUL HOBBIES

In our fast-paced, constantly connected world, the ability to slow down, unwind, and find moments of tranquility is more important than ever. The hobbies we'll explore in this section offer more than just a pleasant way to pass the time—they provide a gateway to mindfulness, self-care, and emotional balance.

Whether it's the repetitive motions of knitting, the focused attention of coloring, or the sensory engagement of aromatherapy, these activities can help quiet the mind, reduce anxiety, and promote a sense of well-being. They offer a much-needed respite from the demands of daily life and a chance to recharge our mental and emotional batteries.

CREATING SPACE FOR SERENITY

One of the key themes we'll explore is the importance of creating a dedicated space for your relaxation hobbies. We'll learn how to carve out a personal oasis within your home—a "Hobby Haven" where you can retreat to engage in activities that soothe your soul and calm your mind.

THE JOURNEY AHEAD

In the chapters that follow, we'll delve into a variety of hobbies specifically chosen for their stress-relieving and relaxation-inducing qualities. From the meditative practice of hand embroidery to the calming effects of observing nature, from the creative expression of candle making to the mindful movements of tai chi, we'll discover a range of activities that can help you find your zen.

Remember, the goal isn't to master these hobbies or to strive for perfection. It's about finding activities that resonate with you personally and allow you to disconnect from stress and connect with a sense of inner peace. Whether you're an introvert who recharges through solitary pursuits or someone who finds relaxation in gentle social interactions, there's a stress-relieving hobby out there for you.

So take a deep breath, relax your shoulders, and prepare to explore the world of calming, centering hobbies. It's time to discover how the right leisure activities can become your personal oasis of calm in the midst of life's storms. Let's begin this journey toward a more relaxed, centered you!

CHAPTER 34

THE "HOBBY HAVEN" METHOD: CREATING A DEDICATED SPACE FOR YOUR PURSUITS

Have you ever felt the frustration of having to pack up your half-finished project because dinner needs to be served on the table you're using? Or perhaps you've lost your creative flow searching for supplies scattered throughout your home? Welcome to the "Hobby Haven" method, where we'll explore how creating a dedicated space for your hobbies can enhance your enjoyment, deepen your practice, and provide a personal oasis of creativity and relaxation.

THE POWER OF A DEDICATED SPACE

Having a specific area devoted to your hobby, no matter how small, can have a profound impact on your practice. It's not just about convenience, though. Creating a physical and mental space signals to your brain: "This is where the magic happens." When you step into your Hobby Haven, you're entering a zone dedicated to your passion, free from the distractions and demands of daily life.

This dedicated space can help you transition more easily into your hobby mindset. Just like putting on workout clothes can motivate you to exercise, entering your Hobby Haven can inspire you to engage with your craft, even on days when you might not initially feel motivated.

CREATING YOUR HOBBY HAVEN

Your Hobby Haven doesn't need to be an entire room (though if you have the space, go for it!). It could be a corner of your bedroom, a section of your garage, or even a portable setup you can easily stow away when not in use. The key is to have a designated area that's organized and ready for you to dive into your hobby at a moment's notice.

Consider the following elements when setting up your space:

- **Storage:** Invest in organizational tools that make sense for your hobby. This might be shelving units, craft carts, or specialized storage solutions.
- **Lighting:** Good lighting is crucial for most hobbies. Natural light is ideal, but if that's not possible, invest in quality task lighting.
- **Comfort:** Whether it's a comfortable chair, an ergonomic work surface, or a cushioned mat for standing, make sure your space supports long periods of engagement with your hobby.
- **Inspiration:** Surround yourself with things that inspire you—artwork, mood boards, or objects related to your hobby.

MAXIMIZING SMALL SPACES

If you're tight on space, get creative with your Hobby Haven. Consider multi-functional furniture, like a desk that folds down from the wall or a crafting cart that can be wheeled into a closet when not in use. Vertical space is your friend—use wall-mounted organizers or pegboards to keep tools accessible without cluttering your work surface.

Remember, even a tiny, well-organized space can be highly effective. The goal is to have a spot where your supplies are readily available, and you can easily pick up where you left off.

THE MENTAL BENEFITS OF A HOBBY HAVEN

Beyond the practical advantages, having a dedicated hobby space can provide significant mental and emotional benefits. It can serve as a visual reminder to engage in self-care and pursue your passions. In a world where we're often pulled in many directions, your Hobby Haven becomes a physical manifestation of your commitment to personal growth and enjoyment.

Moreover, the act of creating and maintaining this space can be a form of mindfulness practice. As you organize your tools or tidy up after a session, you're engaging in a ritual that can help transition your mind from the stresses of daily life to a more focused, relaxed state.

MAKING IT WORK FOR YOU

Remember, your Hobby Haven should be tailored to your needs and preferences. If you thrive on a bit of creative chaos, don't feel pressured to maintain a perfectly organized space. The key is to create an environment that enhances your enjoyment of your hobby and makes it easier for you to engage with it regularly.

Be open to evolving your space as your needs change. As you deepen your practice or explore new aspects of your hobby, your Hobby Haven might need to adapt. Embrace this as part of your creative journey.

As you create your Hobby Haven, you're not just organizing physical space—you're carving out a niche in your life dedicated to your passions and personal growth. Whether it's a crafting corner, a reading nook, or a home studio, your Hobby Haven becomes a tangible reminder of the importance of making time for the activities that bring you joy and fulfillment.

So, are you ready to create your own Hobby Haven? Whether you're clearing out a closet, rearranging a room, or simply designating a special shelf, you're taking a decisive step toward prioritizing your hobbies and creating a personal sanctuary for creativity and relaxation.

As we move from creating physical spaces to enhancing our sensory experiences, our next chapter will delve into the aromatic world of aromatherapy and essential oils. Get ready to discover how these fragrant allies can complement your hobbies, enhance relaxation, and create an atmosphere conducive to creativity and calm. It's time to breathe deep and let the power of scent transform your hobby experience!

CHAPTER 35

AROMATHERAPY AND ESSENTIAL OILS: USING SCENT TO ENHANCE YOUR HOBBIES

H ave you ever noticed how a particular scent can instantly transport you to a specific moment or mood? The power of smell is profound, and harnessing it can transform your hobby experience. Welcome to the world of aromatherapy and essential oils, where fragrant allies can enhance your relaxation, boost creativity, and create the perfect atmosphere for your favorite pursuits.

THE SCIENCE OF SCENT

Our sense of smell is directly linked to the limbic system, the part of our brain that processes emotions and memories. This is why certain aromas can evoke powerful feelings or recollections. Aromatherapy taps into this connection, using natural plant essences to influence our mood and well-being.

Essential oils, the concentrated extracts from plants, are the cornerstone of aromatherapy. Each oil has its own unique properties and potential benefits. For instance, lavender is known for its calming effects, while citrus scents like lemon or orange can be invigorating and mood-lifting.

INCORPORATING AROMATHERAPY INTO YOUR HOBBIES

Whether you're painting, writing, crafting, or engaging in any other hobby, the right scent can enhance your experience. Here are some ways to incorporate aromatherapy into your hobby time:

- **Diffusers:** Use an essential oil diffuser in your hobby space to disperse your chosen scent.
- **Topical application:** Dilute essential oils with a carrier oil and apply to pulse points.
- **Scented candles or incense:** Choose natural options infused with essential oils.
- **Room sprays:** Create your own by mixing essential oils with water in a spray bottle.

Remember to always use essential oils safely, follow proper dilution guidelines, and check for any potential allergies or sensitivities.

SCENTS FOR DIFFERENT HOBBY MOODS

Different hobbies may benefit from different aromas. Here are some suggestions to get you started:

- **For relaxation and stress relief** (perfect for activities like knitting or reading): Try lavender, chamomile, or ylang-ylang.
- **To boost creativity and focus** (great for writing or painting): Experiment with rosemary, peppermint, or basil.
- **For energy and motivation** (ideal for active hobbies): Consider citrus scents like lemon or grapefruit.
- **To create a sense of calm and grounding** (suitable for meditation or yoga): Try sandalwood, frankincense, or cedarwood.

CREATING YOUR SIGNATURE HOBBY SCENT

As you explore aromatherapy, you might find that certain combinations of scents work particularly well for you. Don't be afraid to experiment with blending different essential oils to create your perfect hobby atmosphere. You might even develop a signature scent that becomes part of your hobby ritual, signaling to your brain that it's time to engage in your favorite activity.

BEYOND ESSENTIAL OILS

While essential oils are a popular choice for aromatherapy, they're not the only option. Natural incense, herb bundles, or even the scent of freshly brewed coffee or tea can serve a similar purpose. The key is to find scents that resonate with you and enhance your hobby experience.

For nature-based hobbies like gardening or hiking, consider using scents to get into the right mindset while planning your activities. Diffusing pine or eucalyptus oils while mapping out your next hiking route can help you feel connected to nature even before you step outside. Similarly, the scent of freshly cut grass or potting soil can inspire your gardening plans. A vase of fresh flowers or herbs from your last outdoor adventure can infuse your planning space with natural fragrance, keeping you motivated and connected to your hobby.

MINDFUL SCENT PRACTICE

Incorporating aromatherapy into your hobbies can also be an exercise in mindfulness. As you engage in your activity, take moments to consciously notice the scent around you. How does it make you feel? Does it evoke any memories or emotions? This practice can deepen your sensory experience and enhance the meditative aspects of your hobby.

SAFETY AND CONSIDERATIONS

While aromatherapy can be an excellent addition to your hobby practice, it's important to use essential oils safely. Always dilute oils before applying to the skin, and be cautious if you have pets, as some essential oils can be harmful to animals. If you're pregnant or have any health conditions, consult a healthcare professional before using essential oils.

As you explore the world of aromatherapy and essential oils, remember that scent preferences are highly personal. What works for one person may not work for another. Don't be afraid to experiment; trust your nose to guide you toward the scents that enhance your hobby experience the most.

By incorporating aromatherapy into your hobby time, you're not just engaging in an activity—you're creating a multi-sensory experience that can deepen your enjoyment, boost your creativity, and enhance your overall well-being. Whether you're seeking relaxation, focus, or inspiration, the right scent can help set the perfect mood for your hobby pursuits.

As we drift away on a cloud of fragrant bliss, let's turn our attention to another form of meditative craft. In our next chapter, we'll explore the world of embroidery and cross-stitch, where each stitch becomes a moment of mindfulness and creativity. Get ready to thread your needle and discover how these timeless crafts can become a soothing balm for your busy mind.

CHAPTER 36

THE SOOTHING STITCHES OF EMBROIDERY AND CROSS-STITCH

Have you ever watched someone's hands move rhythmically as they guide a needle and thread through fabric, creating intricate designs with each careful stitch? Welcome to the world of embroidery and cross-stitch, where ancient crafts meet modern stress relief. In this chapter, we'll explore how these timeless needle arts can become a meditative practice, offering a peaceful retreat from the hustle and bustle of daily life.

THE ZEN OF NEEDLE AND THREAD

There's something inherently calming about the repetitive motion of stitching. As you focus on each stitch, the outside world fades away, and you enter a flow state. This focused attention acts as a form of moving meditation, allowing your mind to settle and your stress to melt away.

Embroidery and cross-stitch offer a unique combination of creativity and structure. The patterns provide a framework, while the choice of colors and sometimes stitches allows for personal expression. This balance can be particularly soothing for those who find completely free-form activities overwhelming.

GETTING STARTED: TOOLS OF THE TRADE

One of the beauties of embroidery and cross-stitch is their accessibility. You don't need a significant investment to begin. Basic supplies include:

- Fabric (usually cotton or linen)
- Embroidery hoop
- Needles
- Embroidery floss or thread
- Scissors
- Patterns (optional)

For beginners, starting with a simple kit can be a great way to dip your toes into the craft without feeling overwhelmed by choices.

EMBROIDERY VS. CROSS-STITCH: CHOOSING YOUR PATH

While related, embroidery and cross-stitch have distinct characteristics. Embroidery encompasses a wide variety of stitches and techniques, allowing for more freeform designs. Cross-stitch, on the other hand, uses a specific x-shaped stitch to create pixel-like images, often following a gridded pattern.

Both crafts offer their own unique benefits. Embroidery provides more flexibility and can be less structured, which some find liberating. Cross-stitch, with its clear patterns and uniform stitches, can be particularly soothing for those who appreciate order and predictability.

THE MINDFULNESS OF STITCHING

As you engage in embroidery or cross-stitch, you naturally practice mindfulness. The act of focusing on each stitch, feeling the texture of the fabric, and watching your design slowly come to life anchors you in the present moment. This mindful practice can help reduce anxiety, improve concentration, and promote a sense of calm.

Many stitchers find that this mindfulness carries over into other areas of their lives. The patience and attention to detail cultivated through stitching can help manage stress and approach challenges with a calmer mindset.

CREATIVITY AND SELF-EXPRESSION

While following patterns can be relaxing, don't be afraid to let your creativity shine. As you become more comfortable with the basics, try designing your own patterns or adding personal touches to existing ones. This creative expression can be incredibly fulfilling and can serve as an outlet for emotions or ideas that are difficult to express in words.

Many modern embroiderers use their craft to make bold statements, create whimsical scenes, or capture meaningful moments. The possibilities are as limitless as your imagination.

SOCIAL STITCHING: CONNECTING THROUGH CRAFT

While embroidery and cross-stitch can be solitary pursuits, they also offer opportunities for social connection. Stitching circles or embroidery clubs provide a chance to share tips, showcase projects, and enjoy the company of fellow craft enthusiasts. Even if you prefer to stitch alone, online communities can offer inspiration, support, and a sense of belonging to a larger crafting world.

OVERCOMING CHALLENGES

Like any new skill, embroidery, and cross-stitch have a learning curve. You might encounter tangled threads, uneven stitches, or difficulty following patterns. Remember, these challenges are part of the learning process. Embrace imperfections as part of your journey and focus on the joy of creating rather than achieving perfection.

If you find yourself feeling frustrated, take a break. Sometimes, stepping away and returning with fresh eyes can help you see solutions more clearly.

As you explore the world of embroidery and cross-stitch, remember that the true value lies not in creating flawless pieces but in the process itself. Each stitch is an opportunity to practice mindfulness, express creativity, and carve out a moment of calm in your day.

Whether stitching intricate floral designs, quirky modern patterns, or heartfelt messages, you're engaging in a craft that has soothed and inspired people for centuries. So thread your needle, find a comfortable spot, and let the rhythmic motion of stitching guide you to a place of peace and creativity.

As we tie off our last stitch, let's turn our attention to another craft that engages our senses and soothes our spirits. In our next chapter, we'll explore the aromatic world of soap-making and candle crafting. Get ready to immerse yourself in soothing scents and textures as we discover how these crafts can become a fragrant form of stress relief.

CHAPTER 37

SOAP MAKING AND CANDLE CRAFTING: THE ART OF SOOTHING SCENTS AND TEXTURES

Have you ever lit a handcrafted candle or lathered it up with a bar of artisanal soap, marveling at the rich scents and luxurious textures? Welcome to the world of soap-making and candle crafting, where creativity meets aromatherapy in a hands-on, sensory experience. In this chapter, we'll explore how these crafts can become a fragrant form of stress relief and a gateway to personalized self-care products.

THE ALLURE OF HANDMADE SOAPS AND CANDLES

There's something deeply satisfying about creating your own personal care items. Soap-making and candle crafting allow you to control the ingredients, customizing scents and textures to your preferences. This level of personalization not only results in products tailored to your needs but also provides a sense of accomplishment and connection to age-old crafting traditions.

The process of making soaps and candles can be meditative, engaging your senses and focusing your mind on the present moment. The careful measuring of ingredients, the blending of scents, and the artistic touches of color and shape all contribute to a mindful, absorbing activity that can melt away stress.

GETTING STARTED: BASIC TECHNIQUES

Both soap-making and candle crafting have multiple methods, ranging from simple to complex. For beginners, melt-and-pour soap bases and pre-wicked candle containers offer an accessible entry point. These methods allow you to focus on scent blending and design without the complexities of working with lye (in soap making) or creating your own wicks (in candle making).

As you gain confidence, you might explore cold-process soap-making or dipped candle techniques. Each method offers its own rewards and challenges, allowing for continued learning and experimentation as your skills grow.

THE SCIENCE AND ART OF SCENT

One of the most enjoyable aspects of these crafts is experimenting with fragrances. Essential oils and fragrance oils offer endless possibilities for creating unique scent profiles. You might craft a lavender and vanilla soap for relaxation, a citrusy candle for an energy boost, or a woodsy blend for a cozy atmosphere.

Learning to blend scents is an art in itself. Start with simple combinations and gradually experiment with more complex scent profiles. Keep notes on your favorite blends—you might discover your signature scent along the way!

TEXTURE AND VISUAL APPEAL

Beyond scent, soap making and candle crafting offer opportunities to play with texture and visual design. In soap making, you can experiment with exfoliants like oatmeal or poppy seeds or create swirled color patterns. Candle crafting allows for layered colors, embedded objects, or sculpted shapes.

These visual and tactile elements not only make your creations more appealing but can also enhance the sensory experience of using them. The process of designing these elements can be a form of artistic expression, adding another layer of enjoyment to your crafting experience.

THE MINDFULNESS OF MAKING

As you engage in soap-making or candle crafting, practice mindfulness. Notice the textures of the ingredients, the transformation of liquids to solids, and the blending of colors and scents. This focused attention can turn your crafting time into a form of meditation, helping to quiet the mind and reduce stress.

The anticipation of unmolding a soap or lighting a candle for the first time can also be a lesson in patience. These crafts teach us to slow down and appreciate the process as much as the final product.

SAFETY FIRST

While enjoyable, these crafts do require attention to safety. Always follow proper safety protocols when working with hot materials or potentially irritating ingredients like lye. Use protective gear, work in a well-ventilated area, and keep your workspace clean and organized.

SHARING YOUR CREATIONS

One of the joys of soap-making and candle crafting is sharing your creations with others. Handmade soaps and candles make thoughtful, personalized gifts. The act of giving something you've crafted yourself can be deeply satisfying, extending the joy of your hobby beyond your own use.

As you dive into the world of soap-making and candle crafting, remember that, like any skill, it takes practice to master. Embrace the learning process, including any "failures"—they're all part of the journey. Each batch is an opportunity to learn, experiment, and refine your craft.

Whether you're creating a soothing lavender soap to unwind after a long day or crafting a festive cinnamon-scented candle for holiday ambiance, you're engaging in a hobby that nourishes your creativity and your senses. So roll up your sleeves, gather your ingredients, and get ready to fill your space with delightful scents and your heart with the joy of creation.

As we extinguish our crafting flame for now, let's shift our focus to a different kind of creative expression. In our next chapter, we'll explore the world of improv and comedy classes, where laughter becomes a powerful tool for stress relief and personal growth. Get ready to unleash your inner comedian and discover the joy of spontaneous creativity!

CHAPTER 38

THE "LAUGHTER LIFT" OF IMPROV AND COMEDY CLASSES

Have you ever marveled at the quick wit of comedians or the seamless interactions of improv performers? Welcome to the world of improv and comedy classes, where laughter isn't just the best medicine—it's a powerful tool for personal growth, stress relief, and unbridled joy. In this chapter, we'll explore how stepping into the spotlight can lift your spirits and transform your approach to life's challenges.

THE POWER OF YES, AND...

At the heart of improv lies the principle of "Yes, and..." This simple concept encourages participants to accept and build upon their fellow performers' ideas. It's a technique that has value far beyond the stage. Embracing it as a life philosophy promotes positivity, adaptability, and collaboration. By embracing "Yes, and..." you learn to approach life's curveballs with creativity and openness.

In comedy classes, you'll discover the art of finding humor in everyday situations. This skill can be a game-changer in how you perceive and handle stress. When you can find the funny in frustrating situations, you're equipped with a powerful coping mechanism.

BREAKING OUT OF YOUR COMFORT ZONE

Improv and comedy classes push you to step outside your comfort zone in a supportive environment. The fear of public speaking or looking foolish melts away as you realize everyone is in the same boat, ready to support and encourage each other. This safe space allows you to take risks, make mistakes, and learn from them—all while having a blast.

As you become more comfortable with discomfort, you'll likely find this newfound confidence spilling over into other areas of your life. Job interviews, social situations, and public speaking engagements become less daunting when you've practiced thinking on your feet in front of an audience.

THE MINDFULNESS OF THE MOMENT

Improv requires you to be fully present in the moment. There's no script to fall back on, no pre-planned responses. This intense focus on the here and now is a form of active mindfulness. It trains your brain to let go of worries about the past or future and engage fully with the present.

In comedy writing classes, you learn to observe the world around you more keenly, always on the lookout for material. This heightened awareness can lead to a greater appreciation of life's little absurdities and joys.

BUILDING SOCIAL CONNECTIONS

Few activities bond people as quickly as laughing together. Improv and comedy classes create a unique camaraderie among participants. Even better, while you're learning new skills, you're also building a supportive community for yourself. These connections can be particularly valuable for those who struggle with social anxiety or loneliness.

The collaborative nature of improv also hones your listening and communication skills. You learn to read non-verbal cues, respond authentically to others, and work as part of a team—all valuable skills in both personal and professional relationships.

STRESS RELIEF THROUGH LAUGHTER

The physical act of laughing has been shown to reduce stress hormones and increase endorphins. Regular participation in improv or comedy classes provides a consistent outlet for this stress-busting laughter. It's like a workout for your sense of humor, keeping your laugh muscles in top shape.

Moreover, the ability to find humor in challenging situations can be a powerful tool for resilience. As you practice reframing situations for comedic effect, you develop a more flexible, positive outlook on life's ups and downs.

GETTING STARTED

Many community centers, theaters, and comedy clubs offer improv and comedy classes for beginners. Start with a low-pressure introductory class or workshop to get a feel for it. Remember, everyone starts as a novice, and the supportive atmosphere of these classes means you're among friends from day one.

If the idea of in-person classes feels too daunting at first, look for online options. Many improv and comedy schools have adapted their curricula for virtual platforms, allowing you to dip your toe in from the comfort of your home.

As you embark on your journey into the world of improv and comedy, remember that the goal isn't to become the next stand-up sensation (though if that happens, great!). It's about embracing joy, fostering creativity, and learning to navigate life's unpredictability with humor and grace.

So, are you ready to say "Yes, and..." to a new adventure? Step into the spotlight, embrace the unexpected, and let the laughter lift you to new heights of personal growth and happiness. Your audience awaits, and the stage of life is yours to command with humor and heart.

As we take our final bow in the world of comedy, let's shift our focus to a quieter yet equally enriching pursuit. In our next chapter, we'll explore the serene world of birdwatching and nature observation. Get ready to discover how tuning into the natural world can bring a sense of peace and wonder to your daily life.

CHAPTER 39

THE SERENITY OF BIRDWATCHING AND NATURE OBSERVATION

Have you ever paused to watch a hummingbird hover near a flower or felt a sense of wonder at the sight of a majestic eagle soaring overhead? Welcome to the tranquil world of birdwatching and nature observation, where the simple act of paying attention to the natural world around us can bring profound peace and connection. In this chapter, we'll explore how this gentle hobby can become a source of joy, learning, and stress relief in our busy lives.

THE MINDFUL ART OF OBSERVATION

At its core, birdwatching and nature observation are exercises in mindfulness. When you're focused on spotting an elusive warbler or identifying a particular butterfly species, you're fully present in the moment. This focused attention acts as a form of moving meditation, quieting the mind and reducing stress.

The beauty of this hobby is its accessibility. Whether you're in a bustling city park, your own backyard, or a remote wilderness, nature is always around us, waiting to be noticed and appreciated. All you need to start is a willingness to slow down and observe.

GETTING STARTED: THE BASIC TOOLKIT

While you can begin nature observation with nothing more than your eyes and ears, a few simple tools can enhance your experience:

- Binoculars for a closer look at birds and wildlife
- A field guide or nature identification app
- A notebook for recording observations
- Comfortable, weather-appropriate clothing

Remember, the goal isn't to accumulate gear but to deepen your connection with nature. Start with what you have and add to your toolkit as your interest grows.

THE JOY OF DISCOVERY

One of the most exciting aspects of birdwatching and nature observation is the constant opportunity for discovery. Each outing holds the potential for seeing something new—perhaps a bird species you've never encountered before or a fascinating insect behavior you've never noticed. This sense of exploration and learning keeps the hobby fresh and engaging, no matter how long you've been doing it.

As you become more familiar with your local flora and fauna, you'll start to notice patterns and changes. The arrival of migratory birds becomes a cherished seasonal marker. The first bloom of a particular wildflower signals the turning of the seasons. This deepening awareness of nature's rhythms can provide a sense of grounding and connection to the world around us.

A SOCIAL OR SOLITARY PURSUIT

Birdwatching and nature observation can be enjoyed alone or in groups, making it adaptable to different personalities and preferences. Solitary observation offers a chance for quiet reflection and personal discovery. Group outings, on the other hand, provide opportunities to learn from more experienced naturalists and share the excitement of discoveries with others.

Many communities have local Audubon societies or nature clubs that offer guided walks and workshops. These can be excellent ways to meet like-minded individuals and learn more about your local ecosystem.

CONSERVATION AND STEWARDSHIP

As you develop a deeper appreciation for nature, you may find yourself becoming more invested in conservation efforts. Many birdwatchers and nature enthusiasts contribute to citizen science projects, participating in bird counts or habitat surveys that help researchers track wildlife populations and environmental changes.

This sense of stewardship can be incredibly fulfilling. It gives purpose to your hobby and allows you to contribute to the protection of the natural world you've come to love.

OVERCOMING URBAN CHALLENGES

Living in an urban environment doesn't mean you can't enjoy birdwatching and nature observation. City parks, green spaces, and even your own balcony can attract a surprising variety of wildlife. Urban nature watching often reveals how adaptable and resilient wildlife can be, offering unique insights into how animals and plants coexist with human development.

As you embark on your journey into birdwatching and nature observation, remember that it's not about ticking species off a list or becoming an expert overnight. It's about cultivating a sense of wonder, developing a deeper connection with the natural world, and finding moments of peace in observation.

Whether you're marveling at the intricate design of a spider's web, listening to the varied songs of backyard birds, or tracking the changes in a favorite tree through the seasons, you're engaging in a practice that can bring joy, reduce stress, and enrich your understanding of the world around you.

So grab your binoculars (or just your curiosity), step outside, and open your senses to the natural wonders that surround us every day. The birds are singing, the flowers are blooming, and a world of discovery awaits your attention.

As we conclude our nature walk, let's turn our focus to creating harmony in our living spaces. In our next chapter, we'll explore the ancient art of Feng Shui and its modern applications in home decorating. Get ready to discover how arranging your environment can create a sense of balance and positive energy in your personal space.

CHAPTER 40

FENG SHUI AND HOME DECORATING: CREATING A HARMONIOUS HOBBY SPACE

Have you ever walked into a room and instantly felt a sense of calm or energy? That's the power of thoughtful design and arrangement—the essence of Feng Shui. In this chapter, we'll explore how this ancient Chinese practice, combined with modern home decorating principles, can transform your hobby space into a harmonious haven that nurtures your passions and promotes well-being.

UNDERSTANDING FENG SHUI BASICS

At its core, Feng Shui is about creating balance and a flow of energy, or "chi," in your environment. While the practice has many intricate rules, we'll focus on key principles that you can easily apply to your hobby space:

- **Balance:** Incorporate a mix of the five elements—wood, fire, earth, metal, and water.
- **Flow:** Arrange furniture and objects to allow for easy movement and energy circulation.
- **Clutter-free:** Keep spaces organized to promote clarity and peace of mind.

- **Natural light:** Maximize exposure to natural light when possible.
- **Living elements:** Introduce plants to purify air and add life to the space.

Remember, the goal is to create a space that feels right to you, supporting your hobbies and overall well-being.

DESIGNING YOUR HOBBY HAVEN

Whether you're setting up a crafting corner, a reading nook, or a meditation space, consider how Feng Shui principles can enhance your experience:

- **Color choice:** Select colors that align with your hobby's energy. Calming blues for a meditation space, energizing yellows for a workout area, or creative purples for an art studio.
- **Furniture placement:** Position your main work surface or seating area in the "command position"—where you can see the door but aren't directly in line with it. This creates a sense of security and control.
- **Storage solutions:** Incorporate smart storage to keep tools and materials organized but easily accessible. This maintains the space's energy flow while supporting your hobby practice.

PERSONALIZING WITH PURPOSE

While Feng Shui provides a framework, your hobby space should ultimately reflect your personality and passions. Display inspiring artwork, meaningful objects, or samples of your own creations. These personal touches not only make the space uniquely yours but also serve as motivation and reminders of your progress.

THE POWER OF PLANTS

In Feng Shui, plants play a crucial role in purifying energy and adding life to a space. Choose plants that thrive in your hobby area's conditions. A peace lily might be perfect for a low-light reading nook, while a robust pothos could energize a bright crafting corner.

LIGHTING FOR MOOD AND FUNCTION

Lighting significantly impacts a space's energy. While natural light is ideal, supplement with artificial lighting that supports your hobby. Task lighting for detailed work, ambient lighting for the overall atmosphere, and even color-changing bulbs can transform your space to suit different moods or activities.

CREATING RITUAL AND ROUTINE

Incorporate Feng Shui principles into your hobby routine. Begin each session by clearing clutter and refreshing the space. This simple act becomes a mindful transition, signaling to your brain that it's time to engage with your passion.

ADAPTING FOR SMALL SPACES

Don't let limited space discourage you. Feng Shui principles can be applied to any area of any size. Use vertical space with wall-mounted storage, choose multi-functional furniture, and employ mirrors to create the illusion of more room and light.

BALANCING TECHNOLOGY

In our digital age, technology often plays a role in our hobbies. Arrange electronic devices thoughtfully, concealing cords and positioning screens to minimize glare. Consider creating tech-free zones within your hobby space to encourage unplugged creativity and relaxation.

As you apply these Feng Shui and decorating principles to your hobby space, remember that the ultimate goal is to create an environment that feels harmonious and inspiring to you. Trust your intuition—if a particular arrangement or element doesn't feel right, adjust it until the space resonates with your vision and needs.

By thoughtfully designing your hobby haven, you're not just decorating—you're creating a sanctuary that supports your passions, promotes well-being, and invites positive energy into your life. Whether you're painting, reading, meditating, or crafting, your harmoniously arranged space will enhance your hobby experience and contribute to overall life balance.

As we conclude our exploration of creating harmonious spaces, let's turn our attention to how your hobby can become more than just a personal pursuit. In our next chapter, we'll discover how to transform your passion into a potential source of income. Get ready to explore the exciting journey of turning your hobby into a business, where creativity meets entrepreneurship in the most fulfilling way.

PART VII

TURNING YOUR HOBBY INTO A BUSINESS

Welcome to Part VII of our journey into empowering pursuits! We've explored creative expression, active hobbies, intellectual pursuits, social connections, and stress-relieving activities. Now, it's time to take an exciting leap and discover how your passion can potentially become a source of income. In this section, we'll explore the thrilling world of transforming hobbies into businesses, where creativity meets entrepreneurship in the most fulfilling way.

THE DREAM OF DOING WHAT YOU LOVE

How many times have you heard the saying, "Do what you love, and you'll never work a day in your life"? While the reality of turning a hobby into a business involves plenty of hard work, there's undeniable magic in building a career around your passion. This section will guide you through the process of evaluating your hobby's business potential and taking those first crucial steps toward entrepreneurship.

FROM PASSION TO PROFIT

Transforming a hobby into a business isn't just about making money—it's about sharing your skills, creativity, and enthusiasm with a broader audience. Whether you're crafting handmade goods, offering specialized services, or sharing your knowledge through teaching, your hobby-turned-business has the potential to enrich not only your life but the lives of others as well.

THE ENTREPRENEURIAL MINDSET

As we embark on this journey, we'll explore how to cultivate an entrepreneurial mindset. This includes learning to see opportunities, understanding basic business principles, and developing the resilience to navigate the ups and downs of self-employment. Don't worry if you've never considered yourself a "business person"—many successful entrepreneurs started as passionate hobbyists just like you.

BALANCING PASSION AND PRACTICALITY

One of the challenges of turning a hobby into a business is maintaining your love for the activity while dealing with the practical aspects of running a company. We'll discuss strategies for striking this balance, ensuring that your passion remains the driving force behind your business even as you tackle taxes, marketing, and customer relations.

THE JOURNEY AHEAD

In the chapters that follow, we'll explore various aspects of hobby-based entrepreneurship. From crafting a business plan and setting up shop at local markets to building an online presence and teaching your skills to others, we'll cover a range of paths your hobby business might take. We'll also delve into the world of freelancing and consulting, where your hobby expertise can become a valuable service to others.

Remember, the goal isn't to pressure you into turning your beloved hobby into a business if that's not right for you. Instead, we're opening the door to possibilities, showing you how your passion could potentially become a fulfilling career if you choose to pursue that path.

Whether you're dreaming of quitting your day job to pursue your passion full-time or simply interested in earning some extra income from your hobby, this section will provide you with valuable insights and practical steps to get started.

So, are you ready to explore the exciting intersection of creativity and entrepreneurship? Let's embark on this journey together, discovering how your cherished hobby might blossom into a thriving business venture. It's time to turn your passion into profit and share your unique talents with the world!

CHAPTER 41

THE "PASSION TO PROFIT" PLAN: STRATEGIES FOR MONETIZING YOUR HOBBY

Have you ever daydreamed about turning your beloved hobby into a thriving business? Welcome to the exciting world of hobby monetization, where passion meets entrepreneurship. In this chapter, we'll explore practical strategies to transform your leisure pursuit into a potential source of income without losing the joy that made you fall in love with it in the first place.

ASSESSING YOUR HOBBY'S POTENTIAL

Not every hobby is ripe for monetization, and that's okay. The first step is to honestly evaluate your hobby's market potential. Consider whether there's a demand for what you create or the skills you possess. Reflect on the unique value you can offer that sets you apart from others. It's also crucial to ask yourself if you're willing to adapt your hobby to meet market needs. Remember, the goal is to find the sweet spot where your passion aligns with market demand.

IDENTIFYING YOUR MONETIZATION PATH

There are numerous ways to turn a hobby into income. You might consider selling handmade products online or at craft fairs, offering services like teaching or consulting, creating digital products such as ebooks or online courses, or even starting a blog or vlog about your hobby. The key is to choose a path that not only has profit potential but also resonates with your personal goals and lifestyle preferences. Don't be afraid to explore multiple avenues—many successful hobby businesses combine different income streams.

BUILDING YOUR SKILLS AND KNOWLEDGE

Transitioning from hobbyist to entrepreneur often requires leveling up your skills. This might mean perfecting your craft to ensure consistently high-quality output, learning business basics like pricing and marketing, or understanding the legal requirements for your chosen business model. Consider investing in courses or seeking mentorship to fill knowledge gaps. Remember, you're not just indulging in a hobby anymore—you're laying the foundation for a potential business.

CREATING YOUR BRAND

Your hobby business is an extension of you, so let your personality shine through in your branding. Develop a unique voice and aesthetic that reflects your passion and appeals to your target audience. This could involve crafting a compelling origin story, designing a memorable logo, or establishing a consistent presence across social media platforms. Authenticity is key—let customers see the passion behind your products or services. Your enthusiasm can be your most powerful marketing tool.

STARTING SMALL AND SCALING SMART

It's tempting to dive in headfirst, but starting small allows you to test the waters without overwhelming yourself. Begin with a limited product line or service offering, a simple website or social media presence, and perhaps local markets or online platforms with built-in audiences. You can gradually expand your offerings and reach as you gain traction and confidence. This approach allows you to learn and adapt with minimal risk, setting a solid foundation for future growth.

BALANCING PASSION AND BUSINESS

One of the biggest challenges in monetizing a hobby is maintaining your love for the activity. To keep the spark alive, set boundaries to ensure you still have time to enjoy your hobby purely for pleasure. Consider delegating or outsourcing tasks that drain your enthusiasm. Regularly reconnect with what drew you to the hobby in the first place. Remember, your passion is your greatest asset—nurture it. If you find yourself losing joy in the process, it's okay to step back and reassess your approach.

EMBRACING THE LEARNING CURVE

Transforming a hobby into a business is a journey filled with learning opportunities. Embrace mistakes as valuable lessons and celebrate small victories along the way. Join online communities or local business groups to connect with others on similar paths—their support and insights can be invaluable. Don't be discouraged by setbacks. Every successful entrepreneur has faced challenges. Your ability to learn, adapt, and persevere will be critical to your success.

As you embark on your "Passion to Profit" journey, remember that success isn't just measured in dollars. The ability to share your passion with others, the personal growth you'll experience, and the joy of creating something uniquely yours are all part of the reward. Whether you're crafting artisanal soaps, teaching guitar lessons, or sharing your gardening expertise, you're not just building a business— you're cultivating a lifestyle that aligns with your passions and values.

So, are you ready to take that first step from hobbyist to entrepreneur? Remember, every successful business starts with a single idea and the courage to pursue it. Your passion has the potential to become your profession—it's time to let it shine!

As we move forward on this entrepreneurial path, our next chapter will explore a practical first step for many hobby businesses: selling at craft fairs and markets. Get ready to discover the "Craft Fair Cash" method, where we'll learn how to successfully showcase and sell your creations in person. It's time to bring your passion to the people and turn your creative pursuits into profitable ventures!

CHAPTER 42

THE "CRAFT FAIR CASH" METHOD: SELLING YOUR CREATIONS AT MARKETS AND FESTIVALS

Have you ever walked through a bustling craft fair, admiring the array of handmade goods and wondering if your creations could find a place there? Welcome to the world of craft fairs and markets, where artisans and hobbyists alike transform their passion into profit. In this chapter, we'll explore how to successfully showcase and sell your creations in person, turning your craft fair experience into a rewarding venture.

PREPARING FOR YOUR DEBUT

Before you set up your first booth, it's crucial to do your homework. Research local craft fairs, farmers markets, and festivals that align with your products. Consider factors like the event's target audience, vendor fees, and potential foot traffic. Start with smaller, local events to gain experience before venturing into larger, more competitive fairs.

Once you've chosen your events, focus on creating a cohesive product line. While variety can be appealing, a clear theme or style helps establish your brand identity. Ensure you have enough inventory to last the entire event, including popular items at various price points to cater to different customer budgets.

CRAFTING AN EYE-CATCHING DISPLAY

Your booth is your storefront, and first impressions matter. Invest in a professional-looking tent or table covering that complements your brand colors. Create varying heights in your display to draw the eye and make efficient use of space. Consider using props or creative packaging that enhance your products' appeal and tell your brand story.

Clearly display your prices—customers are more likely to make a purchase when they don't have to ask about costs. Also, don't forget to prominently feature your business name and logo. This helps with brand recognition and makes it easier for satisfied customers to find you again.

MASTERING THE ART OF THE SALE

Selling in person requires a different skill set than online transactions. Practice a friendly, approachable demeanor and a brief pitch that explains what makes your products unique. Be prepared to answer questions about your creation process—many craft fair attendees value the story behind handmade items.

Engage with browsers, but be mindful not to hover or pressure. A simple "Let me know if you have any questions" can open the door for interaction without being pushy. Remember, your passion for your craft can be contagious—let it shine through in your interactions.

PRICING FOR PROFIT

Determining the right price point for craft fairs can be tricky. Consider your materials cost, time invested, and the event's audience. While it's tempting to underprice to make sales, remember that your work has value. Factor in the cost of attending the fair, including booth fees and travel expenses.

Offering a range of price points can help maximize sales. Consider creating some lower-priced items to serve as entry points for new customers, alongside your higher-end pieces. Bundle deals or "show specials" can also entice buyers and increase your average sale amount.

LEARNING FROM EACH EXPERIENCE

Every craft fair is a learning opportunity. Pay attention to which products generate the most interest and which display arrangements catch people's eyes. Don't be discouraged if your first few events aren't as successful as you hoped—use these experiences to refine your approach.

After each fair, take time to review your sales, customer feedback, and overall experience. What worked well? What could be improved? This reflection will help you continually enhance your craft fair strategy.

BUILDING CUSTOMER RELATIONSHIPS

Craft fairs offer a unique opportunity to connect directly with your customers. Collect email addresses for a mailing list to keep in touch about future events or new products. Consider offering loyalty cards or referral discounts to encourage repeat business.

Don't forget to network with fellow vendors as well. They can be a valuable source of information about other events. They can even become collaborators or mentors in your craft business journey.

As you embrace the "Craft Fair Cash" method, remember that success goes beyond just making sales. You're building a brand, connecting with your community, and sharing your passion with the world. Each fair is a step in your entrepreneurial journey, helping you refine your products, your marketing, and your business acumen.

So, are you ready to take your creations to the people? Pack up your booth, put on your best smile, and get ready to turn your craft into cash. The world of craft fairs awaits, full of opportunities to showcase your talents and build a thriving business around your passion.

Let's turn our attention to the digital marketplace. In our next chapter, we'll explore how to expand your reach beyond physical markets by setting up an online shop. Get ready to discover the world of e-commerce and learn how to showcase your creations to a global audience. It's time to take your hobby business to the next level in the virtual realm!

CHAPTER 43

ONLINE ENTREPRENEURSHIP: SETTING UP AN ETSY SHOP OR WEBSITE FOR YOUR HOBBY BUSINESS

Have you ever dreamed of showcasing your handmade creations to the world, reaching customers far beyond your local craft fair? Welcome to the exciting realm of online entrepreneurship, where your hobby can blossom into a global business. In this chapter, we'll explore how to set up and run a successful online shop, whether through platforms like Etsy or your own website.

CHOOSING YOUR ONLINE HOME

The first step in your digital journey is deciding where to set up shop. Etsy, a popular marketplace for handmade and vintage items, offers a ready-made platform with a built-in audience. It's user-friendly and perfect for beginners. However, you'll face competition, pay a fee on every transaction, and have less control over your brand presentation.

Alternatively, creating your own website gives you complete control over your brand and customer experience. Platforms like Shopify or WooCommerce make it easier than ever to set up an e-commerce site. While this route requires more initial effort, it allows you to build a unique brand identity and avoid marketplace fees.

CRAFTING YOUR ONLINE PRESENCE

Regardless of which platform you choose, your online shop needs to capture the essence of your brand. Start with high-quality product photos—in the digital world, these are your storefront windows. Invest time learning basic photography skills or consider hiring a professional for key product shots.

Your product descriptions are equally crucial. Be detailed, highlighting the unique features of your items. Share the story behind your creations—online shoppers often connect with the maker's journey. Use keywords to improve your shop's searchability.

PRICING AND SHIPPING STRATEGIES

Pricing for online sales differs from in-person events. Research similar items to ensure your prices are competitive, but don't undervalue your work. Remember to factor in all costs, including materials, time, platform fees, and shipping.

Speaking of shipping, develop a clear, fair shipping policy. Consider offering free shipping on orders over a certain amount to encourage larger purchases. Be transparent about processing times and provide tracking information to build trust with customers.

MARKETING YOUR ONLINE SHOP

Unlike a physical store, your online shop won't have foot traffic—you need to actively drive visitors to your site. Leverage social media platforms like Instagram or Pinterest to showcase your products. Create engaging content that tells your brand story and gives followers a behind-the-scenes look at your creative process.

Email marketing can be a powerful tool for online businesses. Build a mailing list and send regular updates about new products, special offers, or interesting content related to your craft.

PROVIDING STELLAR CUSTOMER SERVICE

In the online world, excellent customer service is your key to standing out. Respond promptly to inquiries, be clear about policies, and go the extra mile to ensure customer satisfaction. Consider including a small thank-you note or bonus item with orders to create a memorable unboxing experience.

Be prepared to handle issues like returns or damaged items gracefully. A positive response to a problem can turn a potentially negative experience into a loyal customer relationship.

CONTINUOUS LEARNING AND ADAPTATION

The online marketplace is constantly evolving, and successful entrepreneurs evolve with it. Stay informed about e-commerce trends, SEO best practices, and changes to your chosen platform's policies. Be willing to experiment with new product lines, marketing strategies, or technologies to keep your online shop fresh and competitive.

As you embark on your online selling journey, remember that building a successful e-commerce presence takes time. Be patient with yourself and celebrate small victories along the way. Each sale, positive review, or new follower is a step toward turning your hobby into a thriving online business.

So, are you ready to take your creations digital? Whether you're setting up an Etsy shop or building your own website, the world of online entrepreneurship offers exciting opportunities to share your passion with a global audience. Embrace the learning curve, stay true to your creative vision, and watch as your hobby transforms into a successful online venture.

As we click "publish" on our online shop, let's shift our focus to another way of monetizing your hobby skills. In our next chapter, we'll explore how to transform your expertise into valuable learning experiences for others. Get ready to discover the rewarding world of teaching and workshop facilitation, where sharing your passion can open up new avenues for personal and professional growth.

CHAPTER 44

THE "TEACH YOUR TALENT" TECHNIQUE: OFFERING CLASSES AND WORKSHOPS IN YOUR HOBBY

Have you ever found yourself explaining your hobby to an enthusiastic friend and thought, "I could teach this"? Welcome to the world of hobby education, where your passion becomes a platform for sharing knowledge and inspiring others. In this chapter, we'll explore how to transform your expertise into engaging classes and workshops, opening up a new avenue for both personal fulfillment and potential income.

IDENTIFYING YOUR TEACHING NICHE

The first step in your teaching journey is to identify what specific skills or knowledge you can offer. Consider breaking down your hobby into teachable components. For example, if you're a knitter, you might offer classes on beginner techniques, advanced patterns, or even yarn dyeing. Think about what aspects of your hobby you are most passionate about and where your expertise truly shines.

DESIGNING YOUR CURRICULUM

Once you've identified your niche, it's time to structure your knowledge into a teachable format. Start by outlining the key concepts or skills you want to convey. Break these down into logical steps or lessons. Remember, what seems obvious to you might be entirely new for your students, so be prepared to explain even the basics.

Consider creating handouts or workbooks to supplement your teaching. These materials not only aid learning but also serve as valuable takeaways for your students, extending the impact of your class beyond the session itself.

CHOOSING YOUR TEACHING FORMAT

There are multiple ways to share your knowledge. In-person workshops offer a hands-on experience and immediate feedback. Online courses provide flexibility and the potential to reach a global audience. Live streaming classes combine elements of both. Choose a format that plays to your strengths and suits your target audience.

Don't be afraid to start small. A one-time workshop at a local community center or a short video course can help you gain confidence and refine your teaching style before committing to more extensive programs.

MARKETING YOUR CLASSES

Getting the word out about your classes is crucial. Leverage your existing networks—your social media followers, craft fair customers, or local hobby groups might be your first students. Partner with local craft stores, libraries, or community centers to host and promote your workshops.

Create engaging descriptions of your classes that highlight both the skills taught and the enjoyment factor. Use phrases like "Learn to create your own..." or "Master the art of..." to spark interest. Share snippets of your expertise online to give potential students a taste of what they'll learn.

PREPARING FOR YOUR FIRST CLASS

As your first class approaches, preparation is vital. Practice your lessons to ensure smooth delivery. Gather all necessary materials and consider providing supply kits for students if applicable. Prepare for different learning styles by incorporating visual aids, hands-on practice, and clear verbal instructions.

Remember, teaching is about more than just imparting knowledge—it's about creating an experience. Think about how to make your class enjoyable and memorable. A warm welcome, a well-organized space, and your infectious enthusiasm for the subject can make all the difference.

EVOLVING YOUR TEACHING BUSINESS

As you gain experience, look for ways to expand and improve your offerings. Student feedback is invaluable—use it to refine your curriculum and teaching style. Consider creating a series of classes that build upon each other, encouraging repeat students.

Don't underestimate the power of community in teaching. Foster connections among your students through group projects or online forums. This sense of community can lead to a loyal student base and word-of-mouth recommendations.

Stepping into the role of teacher can be both challenging and incredibly rewarding. It pushes you to deepen your own understanding of your hobby and offers the joy of watching others discover a passion you hold dear. Each student who creates their first project or masters a new technique under your guidance is a testament to the value of your knowledge and teaching skills.

So, are you ready to share your talent with eager learners? Whether you're teaching knitting stitches, watercolor techniques, or the art of sourdough baking, your expertise has the power to inspire and educate. Embrace this new facet of your hobby journey, and watch as your passion ripples out to touch the lives of others.

As we conclude our exploration of teaching, let's turn our attention to another way of sharing your hobby expertise. In our next chapter, we'll delve into the world of freelancing and consulting, where your specialized knowledge can become a valuable service to individuals and businesses alike. Get ready to discover how your hobby skills can open doors to exciting professional opportunities!

CHAPTER 45

FREELANCING AND CONSULTING: USING YOUR HOBBY SKILLS TO HELP OTHERS

Have you ever considered that your hobby expertise could be the key to an exciting freelance career? Welcome to the world of hobby-based freelancing and consulting, where your passion becomes a valuable service to others. In this chapter, we'll explore how to transform your specialized knowledge into a thriving freelance business, opening up new avenues for professional growth and income.

IDENTIFYING YOUR MARKETABLE SKILLS

The first step in your freelancing journey is to pinpoint the specific skills within your hobby that others might need. For instance, if your hobby is photography, you might offer services in event photography, photo editing, or even teaching photography techniques. Think creatively about how your hobby knowledge can solve problems or fulfill the needs of potential clients.

DEFINING YOUR SERVICE OFFERINGS

Once you've identified your marketable skills, it's time to package them into clear service offerings. Be specific about what you can provide. Instead of simply offering "knitting services," you might advertise "custom-designed knitwear patterns" or "knitting technique consultations for beginners." The more clearly you define your services, the easier it will be for potential clients to understand how you can help them.

SETTING YOUR RATES

Pricing your services can be challenging, especially when transitioning from a hobby to a professional service. Research industry standards for similar services, but also consider your level of expertise and the value you bring. Don't undervalue your skills—remember, clients are paying for your specialized knowledge and experience. Consider offering different pricing tiers or packages to cater to various client needs and budgets.

BUILDING YOUR PROFESSIONAL PRESENCE

As a freelancer or consultant, your professional image is crucial. Create a polished portfolio showcasing your best work. This could be a website, a digital portfolio, or even a well-curated social media profile. Ensure your online presence reflects the quality and professionalism of your services.

Craft a compelling bio that highlights your expertise and what makes your services unique. Don't be afraid to let your passion for your hobby shine through—enthusiasm can be infectious and attractive to potential clients.

FINDING YOUR FIRST CLIENTS

Breaking into the freelance world can seem daunting, but start by leveraging your existing networks. Former hobby classmates, social media followers, or local community groups can be excellent sources for initial clients. Consider offering introductory rates or free consultation to attract your first few customers and build your reputation.

Online platforms like UpWork or Fiverr can also be good starting points, providing access to a global client base. However, be prepared for competition and focus on what makes your services stand out.

DELIVERING EXCELLENCE

Once you start landing clients, focus on delivering exceptional service. Clear communication, meeting deadlines, and going above and beyond client expectations will help you build a positive reputation. Remember, satisfied clients are your best marketing tool through referrals and testimonials in the freelance world.

EXPANDING YOUR SERVICES

As you gain experience and confidence, look for opportunities to expand your service offerings. This might involve developing new skills within your hobby area or finding innovative ways to apply your existing knowledge. Stay attuned to client needs and industry trends to keep your services relevant and in demand.

BALANCING PASSION AND PROFESSIONALISM

One of the challenges of turning your hobby into a freelance career is maintaining your love for the activity while meeting professional demands. Set boundaries to ensure you still have time to enjoy your hobby purely for pleasure. Remember why you fell in love with this pursuit in the first place, and let that passion fuel your professional endeavors.

Stepping into the world of freelancing and consulting can be both exciting and challenging. It requires you to view your hobby through a new lens, seeing it not just as a personal passion but as a valuable skill set that can benefit others. Each client project becomes an opportunity to deepen your expertise, solve creative problems, and share your love for your hobby in meaningful ways.

So, are you ready to take your hobby skills to the professional level? Whether you're offering graphic design services based on your scrapbooking hobby or consulting on home organization inspired by your decluttering passion, your specialized knowledge has the power to launch an exciting freelance career. Embrace this new chapter, where your hobby transforms into a professional adventure that's uniquely yours.

As we wrap up our exploration of freelancing, let's turn our attention to the digital realm of sharing your hobby expertise. In our next chapter, we'll dive into the world of blogging and content creation, where your passion can become a platform for reaching and inspiring a global audience. Get ready to discover how your hobby knowledge can blossom into a thriving online presence!

CHAPTER 46

THE "BLOG TO RICHES" BLUEPRINT: SHARING YOUR HOBBY EXPERTISE ONLINE

Have you ever thought about how many people might benefit from your hobby knowledge if you could reach them all? Welcome to the world of hobby blogging and content creation, where your passion can become a platform for inspiring, educating, and potentially even earning from a global audience. In this chapter, we'll explore how to turn your hobby expertise into engaging online content that resonates with fellow enthusiasts worldwide.

FINDING YOUR NICHE

The first step in your blogging journey is to identify your unique angle within your hobby. What specific aspect of your craft can you speak about with authority and enthusiasm? Perhaps you're a knitter who specializes in vintage patterns or a gardener with a knack for urban composting. Pinpointing your niche will help you stand out in the crowded online space and attract a dedicated audience.

CHOOSING YOUR PLATFORM

Decide where your content will live. A self-hosted WordPress site offers maximum control and customization, while platforms like Medium or Substack provide user-friendly interfaces with built-in audiences. Consider your technical skills, budget, and long-term goals when making this decision. Remember, you can always start simple and grow your platform as your audience expands.

CREATING COMPELLING CONTENT

The heart of any successful blog is its content. Focus on providing value to your readers through how-to guides, insider tips, or thoughtful reflections on your hobby. Mix up your content types—written posts, videos, podcasts—to cater to different learning styles and keep your blog engaging. Always aim to solve a problem or fulfill a need for your audience.

DEVELOPING YOUR VOICE

Your unique perspective and personality are what will set your blog apart. Don't be afraid to let your enthusiasm shine through in your writing. Share personal anecdotes, be honest about your successes and failures, and engage with your readers as you would with friends who share your passion. Authenticity is vital in building a loyal following.

BUILDING YOUR AUDIENCE

Growing your readership takes time and consistent effort. Utilize social media to share your content and engage with fellow hobby enthusiasts. Collaborate with other bloggers in your niche for guest posts or joint projects. Consider starting an email newsletter to keep your most dedicated readers updated and connected.

MONETIZATION STRATEGIES

While passion should be your primary driver, there are ways to earn from your blog. Affiliate marketing, where you earn commissions for recommending products, can be a natural fit for hobby blogs. Sponsored content, online courses, or digital products like e-books can also provide income streams. Always ensure that monetization efforts align with your blog's values and your audience's needs.

BALANCING BLOGGING AND HOBBY TIME

As your blog grows, it's crucial to maintain a balance between creating content and actually engaging in your hobby. Set a realistic posting schedule that allows you ample time to pursue your craft. Your hands-on experiences will continue to fuel your content and keep your passion alive.

EVOLVING WITH YOUR AUDIENCE

Stay attuned to your readers' interests and needs. Use comments, emails, and social media interactions to gauge what content resonates most. Be open to evolving your blog's focus as your own skills and interests develop within your hobby. Your growth journey can become an engaging narrative for your readers to follow.

As you embark on your blogging journey, remember that success in the online world often comes gradually. Celebrate small milestones—your first comment, your 100th subscriber, or the day a post goes viral. Each of these moments is a testament to the value you're providing and the community you're building around your shared passion.

Your hobby blog has the potential to become more than just a personal outlet—it can be a source of inspiration, a valuable resource, and a gathering place for like-minded enthusiasts from around the globe. By sharing your knowledge and experiences, you're not only enriching your own hobby journey but also nurturing and growing the broader community around your craft.

As we conclude this chapter and our exploration of turning hobbies into fulfilling pursuits, let's take a moment to reflect on the incredible journey we've undertaken. From discovering new passions to transforming them into potential careers, we've uncovered myriad ways that hobbies can enrich our lives, foster personal growth, and even provide new avenues for income. In our final thoughts, we'll bring together the key insights from our adventure and consider how embracing our passions can lead to a more balanced, joyful, and empowered life. Let's celebrate the transformative power of hobbies and look ahead to the exciting possibilities that await when we fully embrace our creative pursuits.

CONCLUSION

As we reach the end of our journey through the world of empowering pursuits, it's time to take a moment to reflect on the incredible adventure we've shared. From exploring creative expressions to discovering the joy of active hobbies, from diving into intellectual pursuits to forging meaningful connections through social activities, we've uncovered a wealth of ways to enrich our lives and nurture our souls.

EMBRACING THE JOURNEY: HOW HOBBIES ENRICH AND EMPOWER WOMEN'S LIVES

Throughout this book, we've explored 46 different hobbies and pursuits, each offering its own unique benefits and opportunities for growth. But beyond the specific activities, we've uncovered something far more valuable: the transformative power of passion and purposeful leisure.

Hobbies are more than just ways to pass the time. They're gateways to self-discovery, vehicles for personal growth, and bridges to meaningful connections. As women, we often find ourselves juggling multiple roles and responsibilities, leaving little time for personal pursuits. But what we've learned is that making space for hobbies isn't selfish or frivolous—it's essential for our well-being and empowerment.

When we engage in activities we love, we tap into wells of creativity and strength we might not have known we possessed. The artist who discovers her voice through painting, the runner who pushes her limits on the trail, the gardener who nurtures life from tiny seeds—each is growing, learning, and becoming more fully herself through her chosen pursuit.

Hobbies provide us with a sense of identity outside of our roles as mothers, partners, or professionals. They remind us that we are multifaceted beings with the capacity for joy, growth, and achievement in various areas of life. This sense of identity and accomplishment spills over into other aspects of our lives, boosting our confidence and resilience.

Moreover, hobbies offer us a crucial outlet for stress relief and self-care. In a world that often demands our constant attention and energy, our hobbies provide a sanctuary where we can recharge and reconnect with ourselves. Whether it's the meditative focus of knitting, the physical release of dancing, or the mental stimulation of solving puzzles, our hobbies offer us ways to care for our mental, emotional, and physical well-being.

Perhaps one of the most powerful aspects of hobbies is their ability to connect us with others. Through shared interests, we find kindred spirits and build communities. The book club member who finds lifelong friends, the volunteer who discovers a sense of purpose in serving others, and the crafter who joins a vibrant online community—all are experiencing the joy of connection through their pursuits.

As we've seen in the later chapters of this book, hobbies can even open doors to new professional opportunities. The baker who turns her passion into a thriving business, the painter who finds fulfillment in teaching others, the gardener who becomes a respected consultant—these women have found ways to align their passions with their professional lives, creating careers that are both personally and financially rewarding.

But perhaps the most profound way that hobbies empower us is by reminding us of our capacity for growth and change. Every time we learn a new skill, overcome a challenge, or push our boundaries through our hobbies, we're proving to ourselves that we're capable of more than we might have thought. This mindset of growth and possibility is incredibly empowering, encouraging us to dream bigger and reach higher in all areas of our lives.

THE "HOBBY HAPPINESS" HABIT: MAKING TIME FOR YOUR PASSIONS EVERY DAY

Now that we've explored the myriad ways hobbies can enrich and empower our lives, the question becomes: how do we ensure that these pursuits remain a consistent part of our daily lives? This is where the "Hobby Happiness" habit comes into play.

The key to reaping the full benefits of hobbies is consistency. It's not about dedicating hours every day to your pursuits but rather about making them a regular, intentional part of your routine. Here are some strategies to help you cultivate the "Hobby Happiness" habit:

- **Start small:** Don't feel pressured to dive in headfirst. Begin with just 15 minutes a day dedicated to your hobby. This could be reading a few pages of a book, sketching a quick drawing, or practicing a few chords on a musical instrument. The important thing is to make it a daily practice.

- **Schedule it:** Treat your hobby time like any other important appointment. Block out time in your calendar specifically for your pursuits. This not only ensures you make time for your hobbies but also signals to yourself and others that this time is valuable and non-negotiable.

- **Create a dedicated space:** If possible, set up a specific area in your home for your hobby. This could be a corner for your easel, a cozy reading nook, or a small workbench for your crafts. Having a designated space makes it easier to dive into your hobby, even if you only have a few minutes.

- **Combine hobbies with daily activities:** Look for ways to incorporate your hobbies into your existing routine. Listen to educational podcasts during your commute, practice language skills while cooking, or turn your lunch break into a mini sketching session.

- **Embrace imperfection:** Remember, the goal is enjoyment and growth, not perfection. Don't let the pursuit of perfection keep you from engaging with your hobbies regularly. Embrace the process, including the mistakes and learning experiences.

- **Share your journey:** Consider sharing progress on your hobby on social media or with friends. This not only keeps you accountable but also allows you to connect with others who share your interests.

- **Rotate your hobbies:** If you have multiple interests, don't feel pressured to engage in all of them every day. Create a rotation that lets you touch on different hobbies throughout the week, keeping things fresh and exciting.

- **Reflect and adjust:** Regularly take time to reflect on how your hobbies are enriching your life. Are they bringing you joy? Are you learning and growing? Don't be afraid to adjust your approach or try new pursuits if you find your current hobbies aren't serving you as well as they could.

By making your hobbies a daily habit, you're not just adding an enjoyable activity to your routine—you're making a commitment to your personal growth, well-being, and happiness. You're saying to yourself and the world that your passions matter, that your personal fulfillment is important, and that you're worthy of time dedicated solely to your own interests and growth.

As we conclude our journey through the world of empowering pursuits, I hope you're feeling inspired, energized, and ready to embrace the transformative power of hobbies in your life. Remember, the 46 pursuits we've explored in this book are just the beginning. The world is full of fascinating activities waiting to be discovered, each offering its own unique path to personal growth and fulfillment.

Whether you're picking up a paintbrush for the first time, lacing up your hiking boots for a new adventure, or turning your longtime passion into a thriving business, know that you're embarking on a journey of self-discovery and empowerment. Your hobbies are more than just pastimes—they're pathways to a richer, more fulfilling life.

So, what's next on your hobby horizon? Perhaps you're feeling called to explore your creative side through writing or crafting. Maybe you're eager to challenge yourself physically with a new sport or outdoor pursuit. Or perhaps you're ready to dive deep into an intellectual hobby that stimulates your mind and broadens your perspectives.

Whatever path you choose, remember that the joy is in the journey. Embrace the learning process, celebrate small victories, and don't be afraid to try new things. Your hobbies will evolve as you do, reflecting your changing interests, goals, and phases of life.

As you move forward, carrying the insights and inspiration from this book with you, I encourage you to approach your pursuits with an open heart and a spirit of adventure. Let your curiosity guide you, your passion fuel you, and your experiences shape you.

Remember, every moment you dedicate to your hobbies is an investment in yourself—in your happiness, your growth, and your overall well-being. It's about more than just filling time. You're enriching your life, nurturing your spirit, and becoming more fully yourself with every pursuit you embrace.

So go ahead, pick up that hobby you've always wanted to try. Dust off the supplies for that creative project you've been putting off. Reach out to that friend who shares your interest in a particular activity. Your next adventure in personal growth and fulfillment is waiting for you to take that first step.

As you embark on this exciting journey of hobby exploration and personal empowerment, remember that you're part of a larger community of women who are discovering and rediscovering the joy of purposeful pursuits. Your engagement with your hobbies not only enriches your own life but also inspires and empowers those around you.

Here's to the artists, the athletes, the intellectuals, the crafters, the adventurers, and all the passionate pursuers of hobbies. Here's to the joy of learning, the thrill of achievement, and the deep satisfaction of engaging in activities that speak to our souls. Here's to you embracing your passions and enriching your life one hobby at a time.

May your pursuits bring you joy, growth, and a deeper connection to yourself and the world around you. The journey of a thousand miles begins with a single step—or, in our case, perhaps a single brushstroke, a single page turned, or a single seed planted. Whatever your chosen pursuit, the time to start is now. Your empowering journey awaits!

APPENDIX

RESOURCES FOR EXPLORING NEW HOBBIES

PART I: CREATIVE PURSUITS

PAINTING AND DRAWING

- DeviantArt: Online community for artists to share and explore artwork across various mediums.
- Skillshare: Offers online classes in various art techniques, from beginner to advanced levels.
- Blick Art Materials: Retailer providing high-quality art supplies and educational resources for artists.
- Proko: Offers free and premium tutorials on figure drawing, anatomy, and portrait sketching.

WRITING AND JOURNALING

- NaNoWriMo (National Novel Writing Month): Annual event challenging writers to complete a novel in November, with resources available year-round.
- 750 Words: Online platform encouraging daily writing practice.
- Reedsy: Offers free courses on various aspects of writing and publishing.
- Scribophile: Writing community offering critiques and writing resources.

CRAFTING AND NEEDLEWORK

- Ravelry: Social networking site for knitters, crocheters, and other fiber artists.

- Craftsy: Provides online classes in various crafts, including knitting, sewing, and quilting.
- Etsy: Marketplace for handmade and vintage items, also offering resources for selling crafts.
- We Are Knitters: Provides knitting and crochet kits with high-quality materials and patterns.

PART II: ACTIVE HOBBIES

YOGA AND PILATES

- Yoga Journal: Offers yoga poses, sequences, and articles on yoga philosophy and mindfulness.
- Pilates Anytime: Provides online Pilates classes for all levels.
- Gaiam: Retailer offering yoga and Pilates equipment, along with instructional videos.
- YogaGlo: Offers a wide variety of online yoga and meditation classes.

DANCING

- DancePlug: Offers online dance classes across various styles.
- Just Dance Now: Mobile app turning smartphones into controllers for the dance game.
- Steezy Studio: Offers online dance tutorials and classes in various styles.
- DanceU: App providing dance tutorials from professional choreographers.

HIKING AND OUTDOOR ACTIVITIES

- AllTrails: App and website offering trail maps and user reviews for hiking, biking, and running trails.
- REI Co-op: Provides gear, classes, and expert advice for outdoor activities.

- Leave No Trace: Offers education on responsible outdoor recreation.
- National Park Service: Provides information on US national parks, including trail guides and safety tips.

PART III: INTELLECTUAL PURSUITS

LEARNING A MUSICAL INSTRUMENT

- Yousician: App providing interactive lessons for guitar, piano, bass, and ukulele.
- Musescore: Free software for creating and sharing sheet music.
- TakeLessons: Platform connecting students with local and online music teachers.
- Simply Piano: App offering interactive piano lessons for beginners to intermediate players.

CHESS AND STRATEGY GAMES

- Chess.com: Offers online chess gameplay, lessons, and puzzles.
- Board Game Geek: Database and community for board game enthusiasts.
- Lumosity: Brain training app featuring various cognitive games.
- lichess.org: Free, open-source chess server with various playing modes and learning tools.

LANGUAGE LEARNING

- Duolingo: Free language learning app offering courses in numerous languages.
- italki: Platform connecting language learners with native speaker tutors.

- Memrise: App using spaced repetition to help users memorize vocabulary.
- Babbel: Subscription-based language learning app focusing on practical conversation skills.

PART IV: STRESS RELIEF AND RELAXATION

AROMATHERAPY AND ESSENTIAL OILS

- National Association for Holistic Aromatherapy: Provides education and resources on aromatherapy.
- Plant Therapy: Retailer offering high-quality essential oils and educational resources.
- Aromahead Institute: Offers online courses in aromatherapy and essential oil safety.
- Tisserand Institute: Provides evidence-based education on essential oil safety and use.

COLORING AND ART THERAPY

- Colorfy: Adult coloring book app with a wide variety of designs.
- American Art Therapy Association: Provides information on art therapy and its benefits.
- Johanna Basford: Website of a popular adult coloring book artist, offering free coloring pages.
- Pigment: Advanced digital coloring book app with realistic coloring tools.

MEDITATION AND MINDFULNESS

- Headspace: App offering guided meditations and mindfulness exercises.
- Insight Timer: Free app featuring an extensive library of guided meditations and talks.

- Calm: App offering guided meditations, sleep stories, and relaxation exercises.
- Ten Percent Happier: App providing guided meditations and practical teachings from respected meditation teachers.

PART V: SOCIAL HOBBIES

BOOK CLUBS

- Goodreads: Social network for book lovers, featuring user reviews and group discussions.
- Silent Book Club: International community of readers who gather to read together in comfortable silence.
- Litsy: Social media app for book lovers to share and discover their favorite reads.
- Bookclubs: Platform for organizing and managing book clubs, both online and in-person.

VOLUNTEERING AND COMMUNITY SERVICE

- VolunteerMatch: Platform connecting volunteers with opportunities based on interests and location.
- DoSomething.org: Organization empowering young people to take action through national campaigns.
- Idealist: Website listing volunteer opportunities, nonprofit jobs, and internships worldwide.
- Catchafire: Matches professionals with nonprofits and social enterprises for skill-based volunteering.

COOKING CLASSES AND SUPPER CLUBS

- The Kitchn: Website offering recipes, cooking lessons, and kitchen tips.
- Feastly: Platform for finding and hosting pop-up dining experiences.

- Cookpad: Global platform for sharing and discovering recipes from home cooks.
- EatWith: Platform for booking dining experiences and cooking classes with local hosts worldwide.

PART VI: ENTREPRENEURIAL PURSUITS

SELLING HANDMADE GOODS

- Etsy Seller Handbook: Comprehensive guide for starting and running an Etsy shop.
- Shopify: E-commerce platform offering tools to create and manage online stores.
- Creative Live: Provides online classes on various aspects of running a creative business.
- Handmade at Amazon: Amazon's handmade products marketplace for artisans.

TEACHING AND WORKSHOP FACILITATION

- Udemy: Platform for creating and selling online courses on various topics.
- Teachable: Website builder specifically designed for creating and selling online courses.
- National Speakers Association: Provides resources and networking for professional speakers.
- Outschool: Platform for teaching live online classes to K-12 students.

FREELANCING AND CONSULTING

- Upwork: Freelance marketplace connecting professionals with clients worldwide.
- Freelancers Union: Advocacy organization offering resources and benefits for freelancers.

- Fiverr Learn: Offers courses to help freelancers develop their skills and grow their businesses.
- Toptal: Freelance platform for top talent in development, design, and business.

ADDITIONAL RESOURCES

PODCASTS FOR HOBBY ENTHUSIASTS

- Crafty Ass Female: Discusses various craft projects and creative pursuits.
- The Lazy Genius: Offers tips on simplifying life and pursuing passions efficiently.
- Side Hustle School: Features stories of people turning hobbies into successful side businesses.
- Creative Pep Talk: Offers inspiration and strategy for creative professionals and hobbyists alike.

APPS FOR HOBBY ORGANIZATION

- Trello: Project management tool useful for organizing hobby projects and goals.
- Evernote: Note-taking app for keeping track of hobby-related ideas and resources.
- Pinterest: Visual discovery engine perfect for saving and organizing hobby inspiration.
- Notion: All-in-one workspace for note-taking, project management, and more.

BOOKS FOR FURTHER INSPIRATION

- "Big Magic: Creative Living Beyond Fear" by Elizabeth Gilbert
- "The Artist's Way" by Julia Cameron
- "Atomic Habits" by James Clear

- "Flow: The Psychology of Optimal Experience" by Mihaly Csikszentmihalyi

Remember, these resources are just starting points. As you explore different hobbies, you'll likely discover many more specialized resources tailored to your specific interests. Happy exploring!